Peri

Christ Our Life

Confirmed in the Spirit

Authors
Sisters of Notre Dame of Chardon, Ohio

Sister Mary Kathleen Glavich, S.N.D.
Sister Mary Verne Kavula, S.N.D.
Sister Mary Reiling, S.N.D.

Theological Advisor
Sister Agnes Cunningham, S.S.C.M.

Consultant
Reverend Monsignor Joseph T. Moriarty

General Editor
Sister Mary Kathleen Glavich, S.N.D.

LOYOLAPRESS.
CHICAGO

© 1997 Loyola Press and Sisters of Notre Dame of Chardon, Ohio
Printed in the United States of America.
ISBN: 0-8294-0907-6

Nihil Obstat: The Reverend Paul Hritz, Ph.D.
                  Censor Deputatus

Imprimatur: The Most Reverend Anthony M. Pilla, D.D., M.A.
                  Bishop of Cleveland

Given at Cleveland, Ohio, on 1 May 1997.

Christ Our Life
found to be in conformity
with the Catechism of the Catholic
Church by the National Conference of
Catholic Bishops' Ad Hoc Committee
to Oversee the Use of the Catechism
of the Catholic Church.

Acknowledgments

This present revision of the Christ Our Life series is the work of countless people. In particular, we acknowledge and thank the following for their roles in the project:

- The Sisters of Notre Dame who supported the production of the Christ Our Life series, especially Sister Mary Joell Overman, S.N.D.; Sister Mary Frances Murray, S.N.D.; and Sister Mary Margaret Hess, S.N.D.
- The Sisters of Notre Dame who over the past twenty years have shaped, written, and edited editions of the Christ Our Life series, in particular Sister Mary de Angelis Bothwell, S.N.D., the former editor
- Those who worked on different stages involved in producing this edition, especially Sister Mary Julie Boehnlein, S.N.D.; Sister Linda Marie Gecewicz, S.N.D.; Sister Mary Beth Gray, S.N.D.; Sister Joanmarie Harks, S.N.D.; Sister Mary Andrew Miller, S.N.D.; Sister Mary Agnes O'Malley, S.N.D.; Sister Mary Catherine Rennecker, S.N.D.; and Sister Mary St. Jude Weisensell, S.N.D.
- Those catechists, directors of religious education, priests, parents, students, and others who responded to surveys, returned evaluation forms, wrote letters, or participated in interviews to help improve the series

Scripture selections are taken from *The New American Bible,* copyright © 1991, 1986, 1970 by the Confraternity of Christian Doctrine, Washington, D.C., and are used by license of copyright owner. All rights reserved.

Excerpts from THE JERUSALEM BIBLE, copyright © 1966 by Darton, Longman & Todd, Ltd., and Doubleday, a division of Bantam Doubleday Dell Publishing Group, Inc. Reprinted by Permission.

Excerpts from the English translation of *Rite of Confirmation,* Second Edition © 1975, International Committee on English in the Liturgy, Inc. (ICEL); excerpts from the English translation of *Rite of Penance* © 1974, ICEL; excerpts from the English translation of *The Roman Missal* © 1973, ICEL; the English translations of Angelus, Memorare, Regina Caeli, and Come, Holy Spirit from *A Book of Prayers* © 1982, ICEL. All rights reserved.

Photographs

©AP/Wide World Photos (p. 77); ©CLEO Photography (pp. 36, 38, 46, 47, 58, 103); ©Corel Corporation (pp. 61, 75, 93); ©Paul D'Arcy/Maryknoll Fathers and Brothers (p. 54 top); ©Digital Stock (pp. 4, 48); ©Dominican Sisters of Hawthorne (p. 76); ©Sr. Kathleen Glavich, S.N.D. (p. 81); ©Regina Kuehn (p. 68); ©George A. Lane, S.J. (pp. 5, 13, 29); ©Missionary Sisters of the Sacred Heart (p. 24); ©Monastery of Visitation (p. 59); ©Nimatallah/Art Resource, NY (p. 26 left); ©Our Sunday Visitor (p. 57, 75); ©PhotoDisc, Inc. (pp. 6, 30, 64); ©Eugene D. Plaisted, O.S.C./The Crosiers (pp. 9, 17, 23, 26 right, 54 right and bottom, 56, 63, 66, 72, 104); ©James L. Shaffer Photography (pp. 8, 15, 40, 42, 43, 53, 65, 67); ©Skjold Photographs (pp. 12, 19, 33, 35, 50, 70,73); ©Eliane Sulle/Image Bank (p. 92); ©James Tinko (p. 79); ©Eric Wheater/Maryknoll Fathers and Brothers (p. 54 left)

Artwork

Mike Muir (p. 97); Dan Siculan (p. 39); Robert Voigts (all electronic art on pp. 6–12, 15–22, 24, 25, 27, 28, 31, 32, 34, 35, 40, 44, 48, 49, 51, 52, 55, 60–62, 64, 66, 67, 69, 71, 74–79, 91, 93, 95, and all Bible and flame icons)

Cover photograph by Eugene D. Plaisted, O.S.C./The Crosiers
Cover design by Beth Herman Adler and Robert Masheris
Lesson Opener Title Graphics by Robert Masheris

04   05   06   Banta   11 10 9

LOYOLAPRESS.

3441 N. ASHLAND AVENUE
CHICAGO, ILLINOIS 60657
(800) 621-1008

Contents C

Note to Students

"Mission Control to spacecraft! Mission Control to spacecraft!" You've probably heard these words on TV or in an exciting movie. This is the language of the most daring scientific adventure in human history: the conquest of outer space. The brave men and women on a space mission are carefully selected. First of all, they must be people who are totally committed to the mission. They are prepared well for their assignment over a long period of time. In the astronauts' training, two skills are stressed: the power to think and act on their own and the ability to obey Mission Control exactly. The success of their work depends on these contrasting skills.

Long before birth, you, too, were carefully singled out for a mission! Jesus Christ chose you, not to conquer the universe but to be committed to his mission of salvation and, with him, to win the heart of every human being for his Father. He has lovingly called you to spread his kingdom on Earth and then to enjoy it with him in eternity. This challenge is far greater than that of an astronaut.

At Baptism you were initiated into your mission, and the Holy Spirit came with gifts and graces to guide and empower you. Since then, your parents, sponsors, priests, teachers, and other good Christians have assisted you in your calling. You have strengthened yourself for your task by prayer, especially celebration of the Eucharist and Reconciliation. Now you are getting ready to take the next step: Confirmation.

You will use *Confirmed in the Spirit* as part of your preparation for receiving the Holy Spirit in a special way in Confirmation. You will review many of the truths you learned in the past. You will deepen your understanding of how Confirmation is linked to both Baptism and the Eucharist. More importantly, you will see how the Holy Spirit is your divine "Mission Control," helping you to choose wisely and act bravely. You will learn how to keep tuned in to the Spirit's voice and obey faithfully.

As you go through this book, you will appreciate more and more what it means to be confirmed in the Spirit. You will come to realize that only the Spirit of Jesus can bring success to your mission: spreading the kingdom of God. Twenty centuries ago, St. Paul wrote about the Christian challenge and goal. He told us the source and promise of our holy calling:

Now the one who has prepared us for this very thing is God, who has given us the Spirit as a first installment.

2 Corinthians 5:5

1 Confirmed in the Spirit

*Lord, send out your Spirit, and
renew the face of the earth.*
RITE OF CONFIRMATION

The Spirit of God lives and acts in the world:

 In the beginning, the Spirit of God moved like a mighty wind and brought forth light and life. The universe and all living things came into being.

The Spirit overshadowed a young Jewish woman in Galilee, and the Second Person of the Trinity became a fully human man named Jesus.

 The Spirit descended on Jesus at his baptism and empowered him to begin his public ministry.

Later, the Spirit came to the followers of Jesus on Pentecost. Filled with divine power and new life, they set out with courage to spread the Good News to the world.

When you were baptized, this same powerful Spirit came to dwell in you. The Spirit of God brought you new life, divine life. You received the gift of faith: belief and trust in God. You were called and anointed to be Christ on Earth. You were gifted to share the mission of Jesus as a member of his Church. Now you are on the threshold of another great Spirit-event, the Sacrament of Confirmation. The Holy Spirit is ready to work in you and through you in an even more obvious way. But what Confirmation means to you and how it affects your life depends on you!

How well do you know the Spirit? Underline a sentence above that tells you something you didn't realize before.

GETTING A HANDLE ON LIFE

You are at the age when you make decisions and form habits that will influence the rest of your life. You look around at opportunities, role models, values, careers, lifestyles and accept some to be your own. You weigh what your parents and your culture have presented to you and decide whether or not to adopt it. You make yourself who you will be for all eternity. Some people never get around to planning their lives and pondering what it's all about. They simply drift, follow the crowd, and let things happen to them. Their lives are wasted, spoiled.

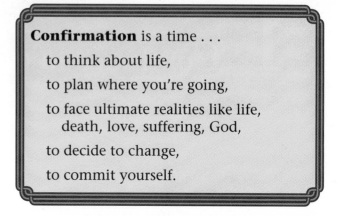

Confirmation is a time . . .

to think about life,

to plan where you're going,

to face ultimate realities like life, death, love, suffering, God,

to decide to change,

to commit yourself.

THE SPIRIT HELPER
Which of these thoughts do you identify with?

- ❏ I don't know what to do.
- ❏ I wish I could be different.
- ❏ What's right?
- ❏ Why am I living?
- ❏ The world is so full of evil.
- ❏ Does God exist?
- ❏ I feel so lonely.
- ❏ Is there more to life than money and sex?
- ❏ After I die, will I still be?

To help us get a handle on life, to help us deal with the problems and mysteries of life, Jesus sent the Spirit. When Jesus commissioned his followers to carry on his work, he promised:

 You will receive power when the holy Spirit comes upon you, and you will be my witnesses in Jerusalem, throughout Judea and Samaria, and to the ends of the earth.

Acts 1:8

Scripture, God's Word, tells what the Spirit does for us.
Complete this imaginary letter from Jesus by
locating the references and filling in
the missing words.

Dear ___Stephany Moreno___,
(your name)

I want you to be my friend and to be happy with me forever. I rely

on you to help others to know me and to live good lives. For these reasons,

after I returned to my Father, I asked him to send the Holy Spirit to be

with you ___always___. This Spirit will ___ you
John 14:16 *John 14:26*

everything. He is the Spirit of ___truth___ who will pour into your
John 16:13

heart the ___love___ of God.
Romans 5:5

When you are ___ the Spirit will give you power
Romans 8:26

and will ___ for you. When you are in trouble for being
Romans 8:26

my witnesses, don't worry. The Spirit will ___. With
Matthew 10:18–20

the Spirit you have power for your ___inner self___ to grow strong and
Ephesians 3:16

to know the greatness of my ___ for you. If the Spirit is in
Ephesians 3:17–19

you, you will have eternal ___life___.
Romans 8:11

The Spirit first came to you at baptism, making you a

___child___ of God. I invite you now to receive a greater outpour-
Galatians 4:6–7

ing of my Spirit and the Spirit's ___gifts___ in Confirmation. All
1 Corinthians 12:4–7

you have to do is ___.
Luke 11:13

Love,

𝕵esus

WHO IS THE SPIRIT?

The Holy Spirit is God, the Third Person of the Blessed Trinity. Like the Father and the Son, the Spirit always was, always will be, and is infinitely perfect. The Spirit is the **Love** between the Father and the Son. It is the Spirit who inspired the prophets and Scripture writers. It is the Spirit who anointed and filled Jesus since his conception. It is the Spirit who makes the Church a community of faith and love.

Jesus called the Spirit **Paraclete,** which means helper (advocate, defender, consoler). The Spirit bears witness to Jesus and enables Christians to follow him and to love, spread, and defend their faith. Any desire you have to do good comes from the Spirit. The Spirit empowers peoples of all nations to work to bring about the kingdom of justice and love. The Spirit renews the face of Earth!

The following names reveal truths about the Spirit. Check the one you like most. Explain why.

- ❏ The Giver of Life
- ❏ The Spirit-Sanctifier
- ❏ Fire of God
- ❏ The Spirit of the Living God
- ❏ Breath of God
- ❏ Counselor
- ❏ Paraclete
- ❏ Spirit of Truth and Love
- ❏ Spirit of Unity
- ❏ Comforter
- ❏ Advocate

Fire and **wind** are symbols for the Spirit. Why are they appropriate for the Spirit? In art the Spirit is represented as a **dove.** Read Mark 1:9–10 to find out why.

A FRIEND FOR LIFE

Ever since Baptism, when you received **sanctifying grace,** God's very life, the Holy Spirit has dwelled within you. The moment you celebrated that first sacrament, you began a new life as a child of God and a member of the Church. You entered into a **covenant,** or pact, with God. The Spirit empowers you to live this covenant and think and act like Jesus.

The Spirit is at work in your life if you can answer yes to these questions:

Do you . . .

receive the Sacrament of Reconciliation?

volunteer if someone needs help?

always celebrate the Sunday eucharistic liturgy?

choose friends who help you live your faith?

practice the works of mercy and help the poor?

take part in religion class and share your faith?

pray and write in your prayer journal?

rely on God to help overcome weaknesses?

read about the lives of the saints?

try not to complain if life does not go your way?

believe that God is working in your life when you are misunderstood?

A CONFIRMED COMMITMENT

Now you have the chance to choose Christ and his Church for yourself. You can confirm your life in Christ in the Sacrament of Confirmation. You can commit yourself to living as Jesus did. *When you are confirmed, what happened at baptism is sealed or confirmed in you. The Spirit and the Spirit's gifts are strengthened in you. You are linked more closely to Christ and the Church.* Through confirmation you come to fulfill the words of this prayer:

> O most merciful Friend, my Brother, and my Redeemer,
>   may I **know** you more **clearly,**
>   **love** you more **dearly,**
>   and **follow** you more **nearly,**
> day by day, day by day. Amen.
>
> *St. Richard of Chichester*

SPIRIT-FILLED PEOPLE

The Spirit has enabled Christians of every century to live like Jesus and become saints. Here is a sample of the Holy Spirit at work in St. Frances Xavier Cabrini in New York, 1890:

"No!" The bishop sighed and looked at "Mother" Frances Cabrini. "No, you do not want the property across the river. There is no drinking water."

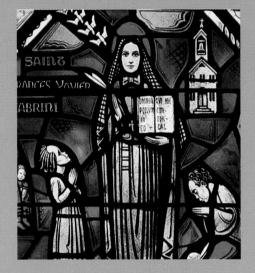

"But, Bishop," pleaded Frances, never known to give up, "the children in the orphanage need fresh air and a place to run. They can't do it in the crowded house on Fifty-ninth Street."

"Where will you get the money?" asked the bishop patiently.

"God will take care. Have faith." The bishop gave in reluctantly. In the next few weeks Frances and her sisters were very busy. They prayed to the Spirit. They went out begging from butchers, bakers, rich friends, and merchants. They got the money, food, and clothing needed. After they moved in, the land was surveyed and a well was found!

The Spirit enabled Frances Cabrini to found nearly seventy institutions for the poor and the suffering. She crossed the ocean thirty times. Nothing stops a Spirit-filled Christian!

The saints were ordinary Christians just like you! They relied on the Spirit and followed where the Spirit led.

FOR CONFIRMATION

A Namesake

You can make one saint your patron for your Christian journey. You can honor this saint by prayer and imitation. Your patron saint will support you. For confirmation you may keep your baptismal name to make clear that confirmation seals what was done in baptism. Or you may choose a new name and honor another saint. In the box, design and color your confirmation name.

I chose this name because _____.

The saint I chose is _Santa Cecilia_____, whose feast day is _Nov. 22_.

What impresses me most about my saint is _____.

I can imitate my saint by (Be specific!) _____.

A SPECIAL JOURNAL

To enter more deeply into your preparation for Confirmation, you will want to keep a journal. In this journal you can record prayers, new insights, the RESPOND activities in this book, what you have done to celebrate the Spirit in your life, and your reactions. Worksheets and other handouts you receive during the weeks of preparation can also be kept in your journal. From time to time, you might review your entries and give thanks for what God is doing.

REMEMBER

Who is the Holy Spirit?
The Holy Spirit is God, the Third Person of the Blessed Trinity, who dwells in us through sanctifying grace.

What does the Holy Spirit do for us?
The Spirit strengthens us and makes us holy. The Spirit enables us to love, spread, and defend our faith.

How does the Holy Spirit give meaning to our lives?

 The love of God has been poured out into our hearts through the holy Spirit that has been given to us.

Romans 5:5

Words to Know
◆ Holy Spirit ◆ Paraclete
◆ Confirmation ◆ covenant

Words to Memorize
Prayer to the Holy Spirit
(inside front cover)

RESPOND

◆ The Holy Spirit has sometimes been called the Forgotten Person of the Trinity. Remember the Spirit by writing a prayer using one of the names for the Spirit on page 8. Include specific ways you would like the Spirit to help you prepare for Confirmation.

◆ The Spirit has been leading you closer to Jesus throughout your life. Answer these questions and you will see how.

Worship: How do the Eucharist and prayer mean more to you now than they did six years ago?

Witness: How has the witness of a family member or a friend influenced you to be a more faith-filled Christian? How were you able to influence someone to become a better person?

Faith: What is one way you have experienced God's love for you or for your family in the past year?

Community: How has your parish helped you to love God and others?

REACH OUT

1. The Greek word *martyr* means "witness." Reflect on how you have lived your faith in difficult times. Name three ways you have given witness to Christ and the Gospel this past week.

2. Preparing for Confirmation involves hearing the stories of other Christians. Interview priests, teachers, members of your parish community, and members of your family. Ask them about people and events that have influenced their faith lives. Make a "Christian Witness Book" from what you heard.

3. Collect prayers and/or hymns to the Holy Spirit. Report on three new things they reveal to you about the Spirit.

4. Read the scripture account of one of the Spirit-events listed at the top of page 6. Tell someone about the event. (Creation—Genesis 1; Incarnation—Luke 1:26–38; Baptism—John 3:1–8; Pentecost—Acts 2:1–4)

A Secret Message Cross out the first letter and then every other letter. The remaining letters spell four words that tell what the Spirit is for you. List them.

J H E E S L U P S
E C R H C R O I
U S N T S S E O L
N O O R F C M O
A M R F Y O I R
S T L E O R R S D
A A N N C D T S I
A F V I I E O R R

_____ _____

_____ _____

Can you find a hidden sentence in the puzzle made by the crossed out letters? Write it here:

_____

_____

S.O.S.: Send Out the Spirit!   Complete the acrostic.

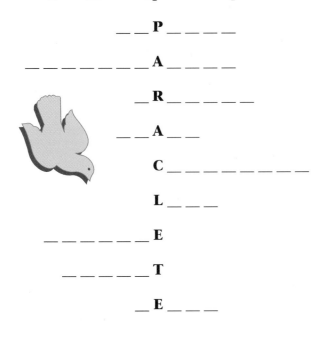

__ __ P __ __ __ __

__ __ __ __ __ __ __ A __ __ __ __

__ R __ __ __ __ __ __

__ __ A __ __

C __ __ __ __ __ __ __ __

L __ __ __

__ __ __ __ __ E

__ __ __ __ __ __ T

__ E __ __ __

◆ The Holy Spirit came to dwell in you at _____ .

◆ Your commitment as a Christian is sealed at _____ .

◆ The Holy Spirit is the Third Person of the Blessed _____ .

◆ The Spirit _____ within you. (Romans 8:26–27)

◆ At baptism you became a child of God and a _____ .

◆ The _____ of God is poured into your heart by the Holy Spirit.

◆ The Spirit gives Christians the _____ to proclaim the Word and to witness.

◆ The Spirit works to make you holy, like _____ .

◆ The Spirit enables you to use your gifts to _____ those who are in need.

Confirming the Facts!   Circle the best answer.

1. Who is the Holy Spirit?   a dove   (God)   an angel

2. What is a paraclete?   (a helper)   a saint   a confirmed person

3. What is the Spirit in the Trinity?   (Love between the Father and Son)   Faith   Knowledge

4. When does the Spirit first come to us?   at birth   (at baptism)   at confirmation

5. What is a symbol of the Spirit?   water   (fire)   hands

6. When did the Spirit first come to the Church?   Good Friday   the Ascension   Pentecost

7. What gift did we first receive at baptism?   faith   holy water   (God's love)

8. What does "sealed" mean?   baptized   (confirmed)   written

Celebration: Receiving the Gospel

Leader: The Lord be with you.

All: And also with you.

Leader: What do you ask of God's Church?

Candidates: We want to be renewed in the Holy Spirit so we can live like Jesus and be faithful members of the Church. We ask to prepare for our confirmation.

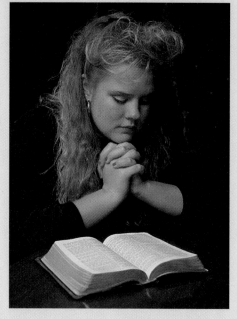

Leader: Do you promise to be active in the Christian community, to be faithful in celebrating the sacraments, and to seek to grow in faith?

Candidates: We are ready and willing to follow the Gospel.

Leader: Candidates, the way of the Gospel now lies open before you. Set your feet firmly in that path. Walk in the light of Christ. Commit your lives daily to his care, so that you may come to believe in him with all your heart. This is the way of faith along which Christ leads you in love toward eternal life. Are you prepared to continue this journey today under the guidance of Christ?

Candidates: We are!

Leader: Are you who present these candidates ready to help them find and follow Christ?

All: We are!

Leader: Candidates, come forward with your sponsors to receive the Gospel, the Good News of Jesus Christ, the Son of God.

(Candidates receive the Gospel.)

Reader 1: That God our Father may reveal his Christ to us more and more with every passing day, let us pray to the Lord. [Response: Lord, hear our prayer.]

Reader 2: That we may undertake with generous hearts and souls whatever God may ask of us, let us pray to the Lord. [Response]

Reader 3: That we may find in our community compelling signs of unity and generous love, let us pray to the Lord. [Response]

Reader 4: That we may become more responsive to the needs of others, let us pray to the Lord. [Response]

Reader 5: That we may be found worthy to be renewed in the Holy Spirit, let us pray to the Lord. [Response]

2 Confirmed in Discipleship

No one can say, "Jesus is Lord,"
except by the holy Spirit.
1 CORINTHIANS 12:3

Have you ever made a pact with another person or group? If so, did it express or strengthen your friendship? Explain.

_____

_____

Relationships are welded together by promises. The deeper the love between people, the firmer their covenant. God forms covenants. In the Sinai desert God made the Israelites his Chosen People in a covenant sealed with the blood of an animal. They promised to obey God's commandments, and God promised to be their God and to care for them.

Jesus gave us a new covenant. At the Last Supper he took a cup and said, "This is my blood of the covenant which will be shed for many." By his death and resurrection, Jesus formed a new people. Those who believed in him, followed him, and kept his commandment of love were his Church. Before Jesus ascended, he promised to send the Spirit to help his followers. The Spirit would make them holy. On **Pentecost,** Jesus' promise was fulfilled.

BIRTH OF A NEW PEOPLE
The apostles and Mary were praying in an upper room. Suddenly a noise like a powerful wind filled the house. Something like tongues of fire came to rest on the head of each one. The descent of the Spirit on the early Church was dramatic. So were the effects. The Spirit-filled Christians went out and spoke in strange languages about the marvels of God. People visiting the city from foreign lands could understand them. They were amazed and puzzled. The Church was displayed for all to see.

The apostles were changed persons. Cowardice was turned into courage, unbelief became a flaming faith, jealousy gave way to love, selfishness was replaced by ministry to others. Nothing could shake the faith of the apostles. They were ready to witness to Jesus to the point of suffering and death. On Pentecost Peter proclaimed that Jesus, who had died and risen, is the Lord and Savior. That day three thousand people were baptized and received the gift of the Holy Spirit. The Church was alive!

A SPIRIT-FILLED COMMUNITY
Guided by the Spirit, the believers formed a faith community with four main characteristics:

 Community—They lived together, prayed together, and owned everything in common.

 Message—They accepted the teachings of the apostles and spread the Good News about Jesus.

 Worship—In memory of Jesus they celebrated the Eucharist.

Service—Their love for one another and for the poor was outstanding.

People who desired to belong to the Christian community were prepared for baptism. Then, at the Easter Vigil, they were initiated. They descended into a pool to signify dying with Christ and dying to their old way of life. A bishop baptized them. Then they ascended stairs at the other side of the pool, which symbolized rising with Christ to new life. On the same night, the new Christians completed their initiation by celebrating Confirmation and Eucharist. Through the power of the Spirit, they were bound to God by the new covenant. They became God's partners in renewing the face of the earth.

INITIATION TODAY
Baptism, Confirmation, and Eucharist are all sacraments of initiation. In the course of time, Confirmation and the Eucharist became separated from Baptism in the Western Church, but not in the Eastern Churches. Recently, the Western Church has reunited them by restoring the Rite of Christian Initiation of Adults (RCIA). In this rite, adults go through a process in which they learn what it means to be a Christian. At the end they are initiated into the Church by all three sacraments of initiation at the Easter Vigil.

The process you will follow as you prepare for Confirmation is similar to the RCIA. The celebrations in this book are adapted from its rituals.

Research your own baptism to fill in the missing data in the "newspaper article."

_____
(name)

IS BAPTIZED!

On _____, _____, _____, became a member of the
   (date)   (name)   (age)

Catholic Church. The baptism took place at _____, at
                                                        (church)

_____. It was a _____ day. _____ administered
   (time)   (weather)   (priest or deacon)

the sacrament, while _____ and _____ were
                              (sponsor)   (sponsor)

the sponsors. Present also were _____ and _____
                                         (mother)   (father)

who will see that _____ lives out the baptismal vows. Representing
                          (name)

the community of believers were _____. As a remembrance of
                                        (others present)

the day, _____ was presented with _____.
                 (name)   (candle, garment, certificate, etc.)

Through the support and inspiration of St. _____ and of the Christian
                                                   (patron saint)

community, _____ can become a dynamic Christian.
                   (name)

Although your celebration of Baptism, Confirmation, and Eucharist are probably years apart, they are closely related. First of all, they are all sacraments. **Sacraments** are outward signs of inner grace that is given to us. They are special encounters with Christ that help us grow in **grace,** divine life. Jesus gave his Church the seven sacraments to continue his saving work and to build up the community of believers. Through sacred words and actions, the sacraments strengthen us and express our faith. We are born in *Baptism,* strengthened in *Confirmation,* and nourished by the *Eucharist.* Once we are baptized we may celebrate the other sacraments.

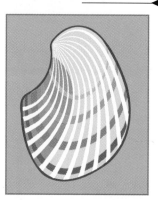

In **Baptism** you first shared in the saving acts of Christ and entered into his Paschal Mystery. You were cleansed from original sin and any other sin and filled with God's life. God came to dwell in you. Your baptism was a rebirth: you died to sin and were filled with new life. You became an adopted son or daughter of God; and you can someday inherit heaven, the kingdom of the Father. Gifts of the Spirit were also given to you.

Baptism marked you permanently as a Christian. The community accepted you as one of them. You share in the priesthood of Christ: his sacrifice and his ministry.

At baptism you assumed the responsibility to model your life on the life and teachings of Jesus. You agreed to profess before all people the faith you received from God through the Church. It was understood that through the rite of Baptism you made promises *to reject Satan and to live by faith in Jesus.* Your parents are obliged to teach you the meaning of these vows. Your sponsors have the duty of assisting them.

Why is Baptism rightly called "christening"?

Suppose that on your fourteenth birthday a rich uncle gave you a car. Although you owned the car, you would need a few more years, driving lessons, and a license before you really could make it your own. Similarly, by baptism your parents gave you the faith and blessings of the Catholic Church. Now the time has come for you to commit yourself to God and take an active role in the Christian community.

It is in **Confirmation** that you pronounce the baptismal vows and are publicly confirmed in your membership. You claim as your own the life you received at baptism. The Sacrament of Confirmation binds you more closely to the Church. It deepens your commitment to be a witness to Jesus, to spread and defend the faith. It anoints you and strengthens you for the mission of Jesus. As at baptism, you are marked with a permanent *character* or seal of the Lord. Confirmation and Baptism, then, cannot be repeated.

Confirmation focuses on the Spirit outpoured on you in baptism. It celebrates the presence of the Spirit within you and intensifies the Spirit's gifts and your response to them.

Only someone who has been initiated through baptism can participate in the sacred rites of the **Eucharist.** Offering the sacrifice of Jesus together with ourselves gives God perfect worship. This mystery is the climax, source, and center of Christian life. Sharing in this holy covenant meal leads us to closer union with Christ and his people. It is the fullness of belonging.

ZOOMING IN ON CONFIRMATION

Words and actions are signs of what is happening interiorly in sacraments. These are signs of Confirmation: chrism, the laying on of hands, the bishop, the cross, and the words "Be sealed."

Chrism

In the drop of oil, write as many uses of oil as you can.

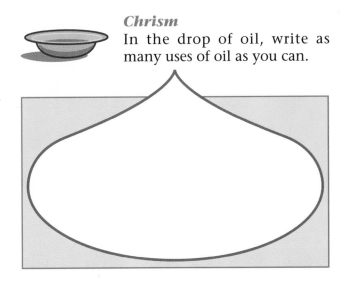

Why is oil a good symbol of the Holy Spirit?

_____

_____

_____

- ✦ Psalm 45:8 says that God has anointed us with "the oil of gladness."
- ✦ Jesus was anointed not with oil but the Spirit. Chrism stands for the invisible Spirit.
- ✦ Chrism is made of olive (or plant) oil and balsam (or perfume). It is usually consecrated at the Chrism Mass on Holy Thursday, or earlier in Holy Week, by the bishop and his priests and distributed to each parish.
- ✦ Chrism should have a strong fragrance as a sign that you are to bring the fragrance of Christ into the world.
- ✦ Chrism should be used generously in anointing and should not be wiped off.
- ✦ In the Eastern Churches, Confirmation is called "chrismation."

Anointing with oil is an ancient ritual to set someone apart for a special mission. The Hebrews anointed kings, priests, and prophets.

Read 1 Samuel 16:6–13. How was young David changed by his anointing?

_____

The prophet Isaiah foretold that the Savior would be the Lord's anointed. The word *Christ* means "anointed one."

Read Luke 4:16–22. Write one thing the Spirit anointed Jesus to do.

_____

The Laying On of Hands

In Hebrew Scriptures, the laying on of hands (imposition) was a powerful sign of blessing. Read Genesis 48:13–16.

In Christian Scriptures, hands healed and called down the Spirit. Name someone Jesus blessed or healed by touching.

_____

Read Acts 8:14–17. Who laid hands on the Samaritans to give them the Spirit?

_____

Read Acts 9:17–19. What happened to Saul when Ananias laid hands on him?

_____

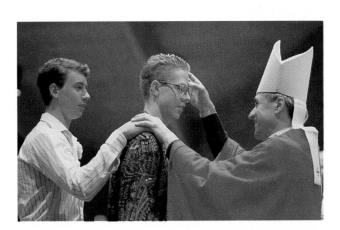

The Bishop

The bishop is the ordinary minister of Confirmation, but he may delegate to priests his power to confirm. The bishop is the successor of the apostles, upon whom the Holy Spirit descended on Pentecost. He is also a link with the larger community of the worldwide Church. A priest confirms with chrism that has been consecrated by a bishop.

What do you know about the bishop who will confirm you?

_____

_____

_____

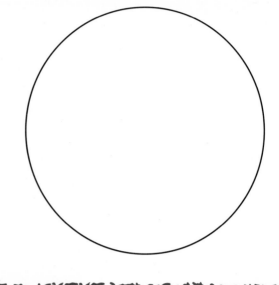

In Confirmation God marks you as his own. Imagine that God stamps you with a visible seal. Draw here what the seal might look like. Use symbolic designs, words, and colors:

The Cross

A cross will be traced on your forehead with chrism. Just as Roman soldiers proudly bore the insignia of their generals, so we bear the sign of Christ.

Check the two interpretations of the cross that you like most:

- ❏ stands for Christ's victory
- ❏ recalls the sufferings of Jesus
- ❏ extends north, south, east, and west, signifying that Christ saved the world
- ❏ reminds us that we might have to suffer
- ❏ represents Christian love: love of God (vertical beam) and love of neighbor (horizontal beam)

"Be Sealed"

The words of the anointing are based on the practice of stamping something for identification. In the past, letters and documents were sealed with hot wax. To confirm that a message was official, a person's seal or signet ring was pressed into the wax, leaving an imprint. Today, documents are still made official by a seal. In Korea people have their own stamps with their names. They use their unique stamps instead of their signatures.

YOU BEGIN

Are you ready to confirm your life as a disciple of Jesus? Are you prepared to center your life on Jesus? If so, during the coming months you will do more intensely what you have been doing all along as a Catholic:

Pray and celebrate the sacraments. The Eucharist and the Sacrament of Reconciliation will increase your love for Jesus.

Try to live the Gospel. You will try to form habits of Christian living and undertake service projects. Interviews with a priest or representative will help you evaluate your progress.

Be guided and supported by Catholic Christians. Your parents, your sponsor, and members of your parish will help you prepare to follow Christ with them.

Study the faith. Through religion classes and sharing sessions with your sponsor, you will learn how to fulfill your vows.

The first step is to choose a sponsor and enroll as a candidate.

A Word about Sponsors

You usually join a club or an organization through a member who introduces you to it. You join the Church more fully with the aid of your parents and a sponsor.

With your parents, list the names of possible sponsors. Consider each one carefully, using these questions as a guide:

✦ Does he/she meet the requirements?
✦ Does he/she live close enough to meet with me?
✦ Is he/she free to attend the preparation meeting and to spend time with me?
✦ Does he/she live the Christian way of life, of worship, and of service?
✦ Is he/she mature enough to guide and challenge me to be a real Christian?
✦ Can I relate well to him/her so that we can pray and discuss together?

SPONSORS WANTED to help confirmation candidates live their baptismal vows. Can be male or female. Must be willing to share faith life with candidate and be example of Christian living, to represent Church by supporting and encouraging candidate, to pray with candidate and challenge him/her to live a Christian life, and to present candidate to minister of confirmation. Must be member of the Catholic Church, at least 16 years old, and fully initiated by Baptism, Confirmation, and the Eucharist. Preference given to candidates' baptismal sponsors. Pay: immeasurable.

Pray to the Holy Spirit for guidance in selecting a sponsor.

Write your sponsor's name here:

What are the sacraments of initiation?
The sacraments of initiation are Baptism, Confirmation, and the Eucharist. We are born in Baptism, strengthened in Confirmation, and nourished by the Eucharist.

What are the effects of Baptism?
Baptism makes us members of the Church and temples of the Trinity. It cleanses us from sin and fills us with divine life, and it makes us children of God and heirs of heaven. Through Baptism, we share in the universal priesthood of Christ and assume all the rights and duties of a member of the Church.

What does Confirmation do for us?
Confirmation increases the life of the Spirit within us. Through this new outpouring of the Spirit, we are strengthened to profess, defend, and spread the faith. We are empowered to give witness to Jesus and to carry on his mission. We are linked more closely with Christ and the Christian community.

What are four characteristics of the faith community formed by the Holy Spirit?
Four characteristics of the faith community formed by the Holy Spirit are community, message, worship, and service.

Words to Know

✦ Rite of Christian Initiation of Adults (RCIA)
✦ sacrament   ✦ chrism
✦ seal   ✦ sponsor

RESPOND

Read over the section "You Begin" on page 18. In your journal write two or three resolutions to help you enter more completely into your preparation for Confirmation. Then write a brief prayer to the Holy Spirit for the grace to keep your resolutions.

REACH OUT

1. Witness a baptism at your parish. As a representative of your community, present the newly baptized with a memento: a holy card, a greeting card, or a candle.
2. Ask an elderly member of the parish community to "adopt" you as you prepare for Confirmation. Visit him or her and talk about his or her faith experience. Ask this special person to pray for you.
3. Make a report on your parish community. Find out how it began. Tell how large it is and who belongs to it. Describe its major activities.
4. Write down your memories of your First Holy Communion. Then write a paragraph telling how your understanding and appreciation of the Eucharist has grown since then.
5. Find out when your parish has a special prayer service such as a novena, Eucharist devotion, Advent or Lenten service, etc. Attend this and worship with your faith community.

A Disciple's Prayer
You might wish to memorize part of a prayer from St. Patrick's Breastplate (fourth to fifth century). It reminds you to center your life on Jesus.

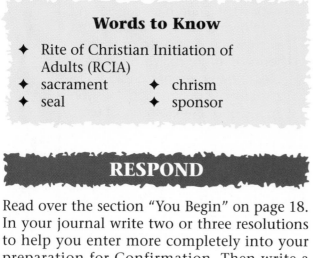

Christ with me,
Christ before me,
Christ behind me;
Christ in me,
Christ beneath me,
Christ above me;
Christ on my right,
Christ on my left;
Christ when I lie down,
Christ when I sit,
Christ when I arise.
Christ in the heart of everyone who thinks of me,
Christ in the mouth of everyone who speaks to me,
Christ in every eye that sees me,
Christ in every ear that hears me.

Witness, Past and Present Write the letter of the characteristic of the Church lived by these early Christians. There may be more than one.

> a. Message   b. Community
> c. Worship   d. Service

_____ 1. Peter continued to preach the Good News despite imprisonment and flogging.

_____ 2. Paul, while praying and fasting, heard God call him to be a missionary to the Gentiles.

_____ 3. Stephen, who spoke the truth about Jesus, was stoned to death.

_____ 4. Dorcas, a woman disciple, never tired of doing good and serving others.

_____ 5. Barnabas sold his land and gave the money to the Christian community, the Church.

Now do the same for these examples from the Church today:

_____ 1. Your parish celebrates All Saints' Day with Mass.

_____ 2. Your pastor is on a Catholic radio program that explains the faith.

_____ 3. Your parish welcomes refugees.

_____ 4. Parishioners prepare a hot meal for the poor after Mass on Sundays.

_____ 5. Prayer groups meet every week.

_____ 6. Adult education courses are held.

_____ 7. The parish social center is used for roller skating, dances, and parties.

_____ 8. Your church sponsors a bloodmobile every summer.

Initiation Initials Use the initial clues to complete the sentences.

1. The disciples of Jesus were initially filled with the Spirit on P_____.
2. The Holy Spirit gave the disciples c_____ to witness to Jesus.
3. In the early days of the Church, adults were initiated with all three sacraments of initiation on the E_____ V_____.
4. Today adults are initiated into the Church through the R_____.
5. S_____ are special encounters with Christ that help us grow in grace.
6. The first sacrament that cleanses us from all sin and gives us divine life is B_____.
7. In baptismal v_____ we promise to reject evil and live by faith in Jesus Christ.
8. One act involved in the Spirit's being given to us is the l_____.
9. A sign of being chosen and strengthened is anointing with c_____.
10. Usually the b_____ confers Confirmation.

Yes or No For each question, write **Y** if the answer is yes and **N** if the answer is no.

_____ 1. Is the Eucharist a sacrament of initiation?

_____ 2. Do many Eastern Churches celebrate all three sacraments of initiation on the same day?

_____ 3. Can you be baptized more than once?

_____ 4. Do you share in Christ's saving acts and in his universal priesthood through Baptism?

_____ 5. Does Confirmation mark you with a permanent seal as belonging to Christ?

_____ 6. If possible, should your confirmation sponsor be different from your baptismal sponsor?

_____ 7. In Confirmation are you more deeply committed to Christ and the Church and obliged to profess, defend, and spread the faith?

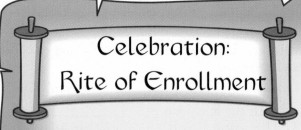

Celebration: Rite of Enrollment

Opening Song

PRESENTATION

Presenter: Father, these Christians request that they be allowed to seal their membership in the Lord's Body through Confirmation.

Celebrant: Let those to be considered for this sacrament be called and come forward with their sponsors.

(Presenter calls the candidates by name, all at once, or by classes.)

QUESTIONING

Celebrant: These candidates are united with us by Baptism and Eucharist. Now they ask to be admitted to full membership in our community. Dear parents, you had your children receive divine life in Baptism. Do you consider them worthy to be admitted to the Sacrament of Confirmation?

Parents: Yes, we recommend that they be confirmed.

Celebrant: Sponsors, are these candidates open to the Word of God proclaimed by the Church, and are they trying to live by the Gospel?

Sponsors: They are. We recommend that they be confirmed.

Celebrant: Candidates, your parents and sponsors have spoken in your favor. The Church, in the name of Christ, calls you to Confirmation. Do you wish your life with Christ and your union with his Church to be sealed in Confirmation?

Candidates: Yes, we wish to be sealed with the Holy Spirit.

Celebrant: Then come write your names in the Book of Enrollment.

ENROLLMENT

(While the candidates and sponsors sign the Book of the Elect, the community may sing.)

ELECTION

Celebrant: Dear candidates, the Church is happy to accept you for Confirmation in the Holy Spirit through the ministry of ___(Bishop)___ at ___(time)___ on ___(date)___.

Candidates: Thanks be to God.

(Applause)

Celebrant: Now we ask God to help you be faithful to his call. Candidates, please kneel. Sponsors, assist these candidates to prepare for the Gift of the Holy Spirit. Please trace the Sign of the Cross on the forehead of your candidate and then place your hand on his or her shoulder.

INTERCESSIONS

(All stand except the candidates.)

Celebrant: These young people, who desire to believe and live as Christians, look to us for an example. Let us pray for them and for ourselves.

Reader: The response is "Lord, hear our prayer."

✦ That our candidates may prepare well to be confirmed and always be grateful for God's blessings, we pray . . .

✦ That their parents may help them to follow the promptings of the Spirit, we pray . . .

✦ That their catechists may always convey the beauty of God's word of life to those who search for it, we pray . . .

✦ That their sponsors may be living examples of the Gospel, we pray . . .

✦ That our parish community may grow in charity and be constant in prayer, we pray . . .

Celebrant: Father of love and power, guide your children. Prepare them to be sealed with the Spirit of your promise. Enable them to share eternal life won through the mysteries of your grace. We ask this through Christ our Lord.

All: Amen.

DISMISSAL

Celebrant: Chosen by God, you await the outpouring of the Spirit. Christ will be your way, your truth, and your life. Go in peace, and may the Lord remain with you always.

All: Thanks be to God.

Song

3 Confirmed in Faith

This is our faith.
This is the faith of the church.
We are proud to profess it in
Christ Jesus our Lord.
RITE OF CONFIRMATION

Because you are human, you are a social being. You enjoy eating, playing, and working with other people. You probably belong to several groups or clubs.

Think of a group to which you belong. What unites you with the other members?

At your baptism you became a member of the Christian community, the Catholic Church—an international body with a two-thousand-year history. You joined a group of people bound together by faith in Jesus and the following of his teachings. Before becoming more deeply committed to Jesus and his Church in Confirmation, you will want to reflect on what it means to be a Christian.

A WORLD OF MANY BELIEFS
The Catholic Church is one of many faith traditions. The chart here shows the percentage of people who belong to the major religions. Each religion has its own set of beliefs. Some are very similar to Catholic teachings; some are very different.

As a witness to Jesus' teachings, you should know and understand them! This chapter reviews the basic doctrines or teachings of the Catholic Church. These truths are contained in the **Apostles' Creed** and in the **Nicene Creed.**

FAITH IN JESUS
Christians believe what Jesus says because they believe in him. They have faith in him. *To have faith in someone is to rely on that person to speak the truth and to do what is right.* You have faith in your dentist, your airplane pilot, your father and mother, who are all human. Think of how much more faith you may have in Jesus, the God-Man who died for love of you.

As Catholics the central mystery of our faith and life is the Trinity. We believe in one God who is a **Trinity** of Persons: Father, Son, and Holy Spirit. These persons have one divine nature and are co-equal and co-eternal, but they are distinct from one another. God has revealed himself publicly through Jesus. Furthermore, **Scripture,** the Word of God, and **Tradition,** the truths handed down since the time of the apostles, reveal God. The truths of our faith always remain the same. However, the Church and you can always come to deeper understandings of them through the guidance of the Spirit, whose help we need in order to believe in the first place.

At confirmation you will be asked if you believe certain truths taught by the Church. The next sections are an overview of these main doctrines.

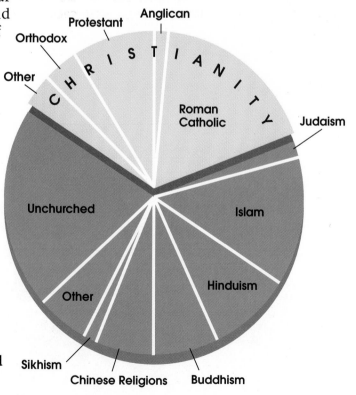

24

> # The world is charged with the grandeur of God.
> Gerard Manley Hopkins

A LOVING FATHER

> Do you believe in God, the Father almighty, creator of heaven and earth?

Who are we? Where did we come from? Why are we here? Where are we going? How do we get there? How did the universe begin? We are surrounded by mystery. As Christians who have the supernatural gift of faith we know a great deal about the meaning of life. We believe in one God, a Being of infinite wisdom, power, goodness, and love. Our God is a pure spirit, invisible and everywhere, who always was and always will be. God created all the marvels of the cosmos. But God is not an impersonal force. Jesus told us that God cares for us and wants us to call him "Abba," Father. As our heavenly Father, God is present and active in our lives. God walks with us, helping us by grace to reach the goal for which we were made: eternal happiness with God, sharing God's truth, goodness, and beauty.

Just as the Persons of the Trinity are one in what they are, they are one in what they do. We, however, attribute the work of creation in a special way to the Father. This includes our own creation in the divine image. We believe that the first people God created, called Adam and Eve, sinned by disobeying God. This destroyed their relationship with God and their hope for eternal glory. Moreover, their first sin, **original sin**, and its consequences were passed on to the whole human race. We are all born deprived of holiness and subject to ignorance, suffering, and death. We also have a tendency to sin. But God moved us from the state of sin to the state of grace (justified us) so that again we share God's holiness. We have a Savior sent by our merciful Father. He is none other than the Son of God. More than anything else, God is love.

In the psalms, favorite prayers of the Christian community, we address God with names that reveal who God is for us. Write the title given in each scripture verse and explain what it tells about God.

Psalm 7:11 _____

_____

Psalm 27:1 _____

_____

Psalm 18:32 _____

_____

Psalm 23:1 _____

_____

What name would you give to God? Why?

_____

_____

A REDEEMING SON

Do you believe in Jesus Christ, his only Son, our Lord, who was born of the Virgin Mary, was crucified, died and was buried, rose from the dead, and is now seated at the right hand of the Father?

We believe that the Father sent his only Son, the Second Person of the Trinity, to atone for our sins. *Jesus is God made man.* He is true God and true man. Jesus was miraculously conceived by the power of the Holy Spirit and born of Mary. She was a virgin before, during, and after his birth. Joseph, the man Mary was engaged to, became the earthly father of Jesus. Because Mary is the Mother of God, she had special privileges. She was sinless from her conception and full of grace (the **Immaculate Conception**). At the end of her life Mary was taken to heaven body and soul (the **Assumption**).

Jesus lived in Nazareth as a Jewish working man. After about thirty years he began preaching about his Father and his kingdom. For perhaps three years, he taught people how to live and he worked miracles. He invited sinners into the kingdom. Envious religious leaders handed him over to Roman officials, saying that he aroused crowds against Rome. Jesus was whipped and crucified. He went to the realm of the dead and freed the holy souls there. Three days after his death, he rose as he had foretold. He appeared to his followers with a glorified body, and then he ascended to his Father forty days later. By dying and rising, Jesus freed us from sin and won eternal life for us.

The resurrection of Jesus gives us reason to believe that all he said was true—especially his promise that we, too, will rise some day. He taught that the bread and wine of the **Eucharist** are himself. Whoever eats his flesh and drinks his blood in the eucharistic meal has eternal life and will be raised up on the Last Day. Jesus is with his Father now as God and Man. But he is also with us in his Church and in his Spirit who guides the Church. Jesus is with us, especially in the Eucharist, which we celebrate in memory of his sacrifice and his love.

At the end of the world Christ will return in glory to judge the living and the dead. He will see that all people receive the reward or punishment their lives deserve. Then God's kingdom of peace and justice will be established in its fullness. Christ will be Lord of all forever!

Read about the greatness of Jesus' love in John 15:13. Write the scripture verse here:

_____

_____

A Self-Test

How familiar are you with facts about Jesus himself? Work this puzzle. If you have difficulty, begin reading part of the Gospels every day.

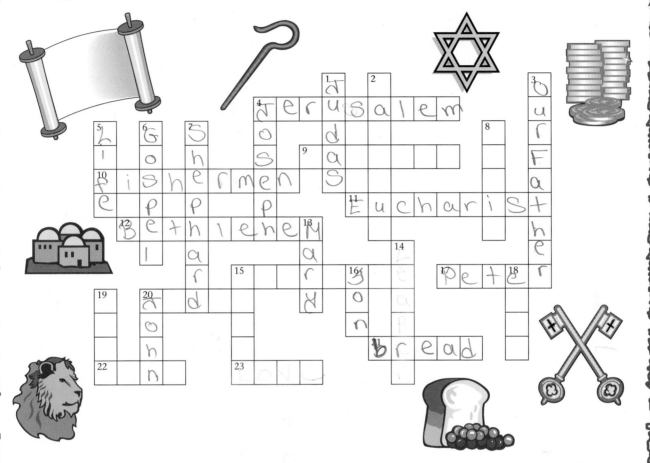

ACROSS

4. Holy city where he died = Jerusalem
9. A story form he used in teaching
10. Occupation of most of his apostles = fishermen
11. Memorial meal through which we meet him today = Eucharist
12. His birthplace = Bethlehem
15. Member of a religious group that opposed him
17. Chief apostle = Peter
20. What he will do on the Last Day
21. Food he multiplied = bread
22. What people proclaimed him as
23. His number-one law

DOWN

1. His betrayer = Judas
2. Friend he raised from the dead = Lazar
3. Prayer he taught us = Our Father
4. His foster father = Joseph
5. Eternal treasure he came to bring us = Life
6. The written record of his life = gospel
7. Guardian of sheep he called himself = Shepard
8. His royal ancestor =
13. His mother = Mary
14. People he cured who were outcasts = lepers
15. Precious object from the sea to which he compared the kingdom =
16. His relationship to God the Father = Son
18. What he conquered and what his followers avoid =
19. One of his evangelists =
20. His cousin who was beheaded = John

A SANCTIFYING SPIRIT

> Do you believe in the Holy Spirit, the Lord, the giver of life, who came upon the apostles at Pentecost and today is given to you sacramentally in Confirmation?

As we struggle on Earth to grow in our love relationship with God and others, it is the Spirit, the love between the Father and the Son, who assists us. Through the sacraments the Holy Spirit makes us holy. The **seven sacraments** are outward signs of the saving action of Christ within us:

+ *Baptism* initiates us into the life of Christ.
+ The *Eucharist* incorporates us more deeply into this life.
+ *Confirmation* seals our initiation.
+ *Matrimony* and *Holy Orders* strengthen us in our life vocations.
+ *Reconciliation* (Penance) and the *Anointing of the Sick* heal us.

Each sacrament gives **sacramental grace**—power to fulfill its purpose. As Church members we are entitled to the graces of these sacraments that Jesus entrusted to his Church.

The original sin of the human race is removed in Baptism when we are filled with sanctifying grace, God's life. But this sin's effects remain in our tendency to oppose God. Often we weaken our bond with God by actual sin, our personal failings. We need to pray to the Holy Spirit and celebrate the sacraments if we are to be faithful to our covenant.

The sacraments parallel the crucial stages of our natural life. They give us supernatural power so that we may live successfully.

Match the sacraments with what they provide.

a. Baptism ✓
b. Confirmation ✓
c. Eucharist ✓
d. Matrimony ✓
e. Holy Orders ✓
f. Penance ✓
g. Anointing of the Sick ✓

___C___ 1. Nourishment to grow stronger in divine life

___F___ 2. Forgiveness after a failing and help to start over

___A___ 3. Birth—the beginning of spiritual life

___D___ 4. Grace for a relationship that will lead to a family

___G___ 5. Courage and strength when life weakens or nears the end

___E___ 6. Provides ministers for the needs of the faith community

___B___ 7. Extra power for the responsibilities of leading a Christian life

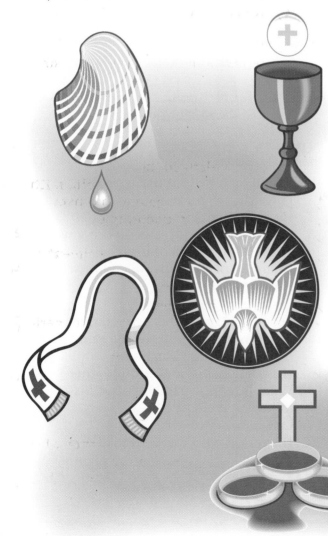

28

THE CATHOLIC CHURCH

> Do you believe in the holy catholic church, the communion of saints?

The Church is a community of pilgrim people on the way to the Father. Basically, the Church is a mystery that combines the divine and the human. She is **Christ's Body,** one way of his being with us until the end of the world. The Church is also a visible society governed by the pope, who is the chief shepherd of the Church, and his fellow bishops. Their authority to teach the Gospel is called **magisterium.** When the pope or the bishops united with him solemnly teach the universal Church essential matters of faith and morals, they are **infallible** (cannot be in error).

Insofar as others share our beliefs, they are part of the Church, too. The **communion of saints** is the Church on Earth, in heaven, and in purgatory. All members are united in love and can aid one another.

The Church has four distinguishing marks. She is **one,** having unity in her doctrine, moral code, worship, and action. She is **holy** because her Founder and Head, Jesus, is divine, her members have all the necessary means for reaching holiness, and she has a holy mission. She is **catholic** because she has the fullness of the means of salvation and because she embraces all people in all ages and all lands, and **apostolic** because she is founded on the apostles and their teaching and is guided by their successors.

The mission of the Church and of each of her members is the mission of Christ—to bring all creation into the kingdom of God. In order to fulfill this mission, the Church participates in the role of Christ as priest, prophet, and king. She worships God, teaches the Christian message by word and example, and serves others.

Here are ways to be an active, responsible member of the Church. Decide which role is being fulfilled. Write *W* if the role is worship, *T* if it is teaching, and *S* if it is service.

1. **_S_** Sending cards to the sick and elderly in the parish
2. **_T_** Studying the Catholic faith and sharing it with others
3. **_S_** Giving support to the Church and the missions
4. **_W_** Celebrating the Sacrament of Reconciliation regularly
5. **_W_** Participating in the celebration of the Sunday Eucharist
6. **_T_** Sharing your faith experiences with your sponsor
7. **_S_** Helping with parish projects for the poor
8. **_T_** Being a lector at Mass

Mary, Mother of Christ, is Mother of the Church and prays for us. Already in glory in heaven, Mary is the image of what the Church is to become.

29

LIFE EVERLASTING

> Do you believe in the forgiveness of sins, the resurrection of the body, and life everlasting?

When we sin, we break our covenant and fail to love God. Jesus assures us that our merciful Father is always willing to forgive. He accepted Jesus' sacrifice for the sin of the human race. He forgives us whenever we seek him in the Sacrament of Reconciliation.

If we live in friendship with God, make decisions in the light of his law of love, and return to him when we have failed, we will be rewarded with **eternal life.** At death our soul and body are separated. Just as Jesus rose glorified from the dead, so we will rise by his power on the Last Day. Our body and soul will be reunited. We will be the same persons we are on Earth, but without the limitations of time and space. We may be with God forever in **heaven.** Those who choose to reject God in life will spend all eternity in painful separation from God in **hell.** Before the Last Day those who die and are not worthy yet to be in God's presence are purified in **purgatory.**

The Church teaches that heaven and hell exist, but no one knows just what they are like. On Earth we do have experiences of joy and pain that give us some idea about life after death.

What on Earth is like heaven?

On Earth maybe going to church could feel like heaven.

What on Earth is like hell?

On Earth maybe being in prison could feel like hell.

We will learn our eternal destination at our judgment. There will be a **particular judgment** the moment we die and a **general judgment** of all of humankind at the end of the world. If we have cooperated with the graces gained as members of the Church, we will be invited to the kingdom of our Father.

GROWING IN FAITH

The precious gift of faith you received at baptism can be cultivated or lost. It will grow strong and bear much fruit only if you study it and practice it. Do you have any questions about your faith? If so, consult your parents, your sponsor, your catechist, or a priest. List as many ways as you can to learn more about your faith and to grow in it.

- _Books_
- _Websites_
- _Praying_
- _Being involved with your church._
- _People that know more than you._
- _Going to church_
- _Reading the bible._

FOR CONFIRMATION

Learning More

See if you know the items under "Things Every Catholic Should Know" on pages 84–85. Skim through the glossary on pages 86–88 and check the terms you know. Do this periodically during this course until all terms are checked.

30

THE CATHOLIC CHURCH

Do you believe in the holy catholic church, the communion of saints?

The Church is a community of pilgrim people on the way to the Father. Basically, the Church is a mystery that combines the divine and the human. She is **Christ's Body,** one way of his being with us until the end of the world. The Church is also a visible society governed by the pope, who is the chief shepherd of the Church, and his fellow bishops. Their authority to teach the Gospel is called **magisterium.** When the pope or the bishops united with him solemnly teach the universal Church essential matters of faith and morals, they are **infallible** (cannot be in error).

Insofar as others share our beliefs, they are part of the Church, too. The **communion of saints** is the Church on Earth, in heaven, and in purgatory. All members are united in love and can aid one another.

The Church has four distinguishing marks. She is **one,** having unity in her doctrine, moral code, worship, and action. She is **holy** because her Founder and Head, Jesus, is divine, her members have all the necessary means for reaching holiness, and she has a holy mission. She is **catholic** because she has the fullness of the means of salvation and because she embraces all people in all ages and all lands, and **apostolic** because she is founded on the apostles and their teaching and is guided by their successors.

The mission of the Church and of each of her members is the mission of Christ—to bring all creation into the kingdom of God. In order to fulfill this mission, the Church participates in the role of Christ as priest, prophet, and king. She worships God, teaches the Christian message by word and example, and serves others.

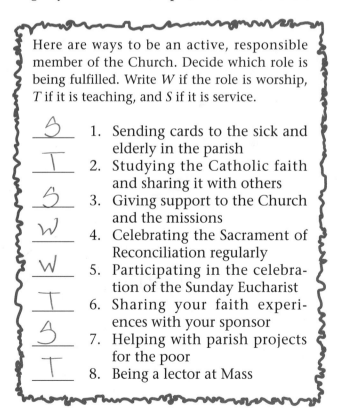

Here are ways to be an active, responsible member of the Church. Decide which role is being fulfilled. Write *W* if the role is worship, *T* if it is teaching, and *S* if it is service.

____S____ 1. Sending cards to the sick and elderly in the parish

____T____ 2. Studying the Catholic faith and sharing it with others

____S____ 3. Giving support to the Church and the missions

____W____ 4. Celebrating the Sacrament of Reconciliation regularly

____W____ 5. Participating in the celebration of the Sunday Eucharist

____T____ 6. Sharing your faith experiences with your sponsor

____S____ 7. Helping with parish projects for the poor

____T____ 8. Being a lector at Mass

Mary, Mother of Christ, is Mother of the Church and prays for us. Already in glory in heaven, Mary is the image of what the Church is to become.

The Church teaches that heaven and hell exist, but no one knows just what they are like. On Earth we do have experiences of joy and pain that give us some idea about life after death.

What on Earth is like heaven?

On Earth maybe going to church could feel like heaven.

What on Earth is like hell?

On Earth maybe being in prison could feel like hell.

We will learn our eternal destination at our judgment. There will be a **particular judgment** the moment we die and a **general judgment** of all of humankind at the end of the world. If we have cooperated with the graces gained as members of the Church, we will be invited to the kingdom of our Father.

GROWING IN FAITH

The precious gift of faith you received at baptism can be cultivated or lost. It will grow strong and bear much fruit only if you study it and practice it. Do you have any questions about your faith? If so, consult your parents, your sponsor, your catechist, or a priest. List as many ways as you can to learn more about your faith and to grow in it.

•Books   •Praying
•Websites   •Being involved with your church.
•People that know more than you.
•Going to church
•Reading the bible.

FOR CONFIRMATION

Learning More
See if you know the items under "Things Every Catholic Should Know" on pages 84–85. Skim through the glossary on pages 86–88 and check the terms you know. Do this periodically during this course until all terms are checked.

LIFE EVERLASTING

> Do you believe in the forgiveness of sins, the resurrection of the body, and life everlasting?

When we sin, we break our covenant and fail to love God. Jesus assures us that our merciful Father is always willing to forgive. He accepted Jesus' sacrifice for the sin of the human race. He forgives us whenever we seek him in the Sacrament of Reconciliation.

If we live in friendship with God, make decisions in the light of his law of love, and return to him when we have failed, we will be rewarded with **eternal life.** At death our soul and body are separated. Just as Jesus rose glorified from the dead, so we will rise by his power on the Last Day. Our body and soul will be reunited. We will be the same persons we are on Earth, but without the limitations of time and space. We may be with God forever in **heaven.** Those who choose to reject God in life will spend all eternity in painful separation from God in **hell.** Before the Last Day those who die and are not worthy yet to be in God's presence are purified in **purgatory.**

REMEMBER

Where can the main truths of the Catholic faith be found?

They can be found in the Apostles' Creed and in the Nicene Creed. (See inside front cover.)

In Scripture, what did Jesus say to Thomas about faith?

 Jesus said, "Blessed are those who have not seen and have believed."

John 20:29

Words to Know

+ faith
+ Scripture
+ infallible
+ communion of saints
+ one, holy, catholic, apostolic Church
+ Trinity
+ Tradition
+ magisterium

Words to Memorize

The Apostles' Creed, the Nicene Creed, the sacraments (Hint: Remember the name B.C. ERAMHO. It contains the first letters of the sacraments in order.)

RESPOND

What you believe influences your life and directs your actions. Tear out "Faith Makes a Difference" from the back of this book. Complete the sheet and add it to your journal. Pray the prayers on the reverse side at times.

REACH OUT

1. Trace your family faith tree. Make a diagram showing how the Catholic faith was passed on to you by your ancestors.
2. Memorize An Act of Faith on the inside back cover of your book by praying it often.
3. Make a chart that shows how we celebrate the truths of our faith in worship. Find feasts, prayers, and customs related to these topics: God, Trinity, Jesus, grace, Church, Mary, sacraments, eternal love.
4. Start a discussion on some aspect of faith with a friend or a family member.

Celebration: Presentation of the Creed

Celebrant: Those who have been chosen for Confirmation, please stand to receive the Church's profession of faith.

(Candidates rise.)

Celebrant: Listen well to the words of that faith which saves you. The words are few, but the mysteries they contain are great. Receive them with a sincere heart and be faithful to them. I believe in God . . .

(All join in the Apostles' Creed.)

Celebrant: Let us pray for these candidates, called by the Holy Spirit to confirm their faith, that they may respond to the love of God by embracing these truths with all their hearts.

(Silent prayer)

Celebrant: *(extending hands over the candidates)* Lord, eternal source of light, justice, and truth, take under your tender care your servants, these candidates. Purify them and make them holy; give them true knowledge, sure hope, and sound understanding, and make them worthy to receive the grace of Confirmation. Help them prepare for that sacrament which calls them to love, spread, and defend the faith. We ask this through Christ our Lord.

All: Amen.

Find the Falsehood Draw a line through the word(s) that makes each sentence false; correct it.

1. Catholics believe in ~~three~~ Gods. *one*

2. Jesus taught us to call ~~God King.~~ *Father*

3. Jesus is God, the ~~Third~~ Person of the Trinity. *second*

4. We believe that all Jesus said was true because of the ~~Eucharist.~~ *Resurection.*

5. Catholics believe that Christ gave us ~~two~~ sacraments. *seven*

6. At the Eucharist bread and wine do ~~not~~ actually become Jesus.

7. Because the Church is founded on the apostles, it is called ~~catholic.~~ *apostolic.*

✗ 8. The pope or the bishops united with him are infallible when they teach the universal Church anything.

9. God forgives all our sins because we ~~made~~ up for them. *confess*

10. There might ~~not be~~ a hell. *is*

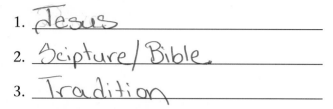

Trios of Truth Write the answers.

Three ways that God reveals himself:

1. Jesus
2. Scipture/Bible.
3. Tradition

Three Persons of the Trinity:

1. The Father
2. The Son
3. The Holy Spirit

✗ Three groups that make up the communion of saints:

1. _____
2. People who
3. Purgatory

Three roles the Church has in carrying out the mission of Christ:

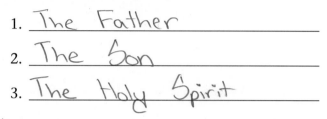

1. Priest
2. Prophet
3. Service

Catholic or Not? Put a *C* before the beliefs that are held by Catholics.

_C_ 1. The truths our Church teaches can always change.

_____ 2. God created us and then just left us alone.

_C_ 3. Mary was sinless from the time of her conception.

_C_ 4. Jesus is God, but not really a human being like us.

_C_ 5. Jesus came back to life three days after he died.

_____ 6. We can live forever because Jesus died for us.

_C_ 7. The sacraments do not change us interiorly.

_C_ 8. The Church is divine because it is the Body of Christ.

4 Confirmed in Love

This is how all will know that you are my disciples,
if you have love for one another.
JOHN 13:35

Actions speak louder than words. Does the way you behave shout to people that you are a Christian? A Christian trying to love like Jesus would do the following things. Would you?

- ✦ Let someone else be the center of attention in a group.
- ✦ Admit doing wrong and apologize.
- ✦ Go out of your way to make a new or "different" person feel welcome.
- ✦ Volunteer when no one else does.
- ✦ Avoid saying anything that would hurt someone.
- ✦ Help someone who is sick or in trouble.
- ✦ Join a picket line against abortion, or for workers who are treated unjustly.
- ✦ Celebrate an extra Mass or a prayer service for a particular intention or in thanksgiving.

 You know what an influence a rock star, a movie star, or a sports hero can have on your life. You adopt their style of clothes, their likes and dislikes, and maybe even copy their walk, gestures, or expressions. Jesus Christ, a Catholic's greatest hero, is the model and guide for our lives. He instructed us to keep God's **Ten Commandments.** He taught the two great commandments:

 You shall love the Lord, your God, with all your heart, with all your soul, and with all your mind.

You shall love your neighbor as yourself.

Matthew 22:37, 39

Then he added a new commandment:

 As I have loved you, so you also should love one another.

John 13:34

How much has Jesus loved you?

Review the Ten Commandments on page 84. Choose one commandment and explain how keeping it shows love:

_____

_____

CODE FOR HAPPINESS

In the **Beatitudes** Jesus spelled out attitudes we should cultivate. They make us more like Jesus, more in the image of God—perfect as our heavenly Father is perfect. The Holy Spirit helps us live the Beatitudes. Each one includes the promise of that happiness we desire so much.

THE EIGHT BEATITUDES

Blessed are the poor in spirit,
     for theirs is the kingdom of heaven.
They rely on God for everything. They are not attached to money and possessions. They share.

Blessed are they who mourn,
     for they will be comforted.
They mourn over sin and evil. They join in the sorrow of anyone who is suffering.

Blessed are the meek,
     for they will inherit the land.
They are gentle people who treat others kindly. They are selfless and serve others.

Blessed are they who hunger and
     thirst for righteousness,
     for they will be satisfied.
They fight against sin and evil and lead others to do good.

Blessed are the merciful,
     for they will be shown mercy.
They reach out to the suffering with compassion. They forgive others.

Blessed are the clean of heart,
     for they will see God.
They do God's will in everything. They are holy and chaste.

Blessed are the peacemakers,
     for they will be called children of God.
They are at peace with themselves, with others, and with God. They prevent arguments and settle disputes. They work for justice, which brings about peace.

Blessed are they who are persecuted
     for the sake of righteousness,
     for theirs is the kingdom of heaven.
They take a stand for truth and justice even when they are attacked by others.

Matthew 5:3–10

A Blueprint for Life Write a Beatitude attitude in each space, using the letters as clues.

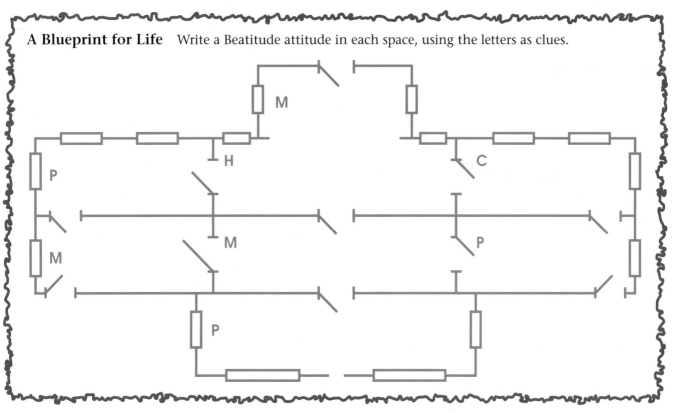

CHRIST IN THE CLASSROOM

In the story below, underline the lines that show Joe living out the Beatitudes. Be ready to explain your choices.

The morning of election day Joe prayed to become class president. He asked God for the gifts he knew he lacked for the job. Cringing, he recalled the mean trick played on Sue yesterday. Bob had put gum on the unpopular girl's chair. When Sue sat down, the gum stuck to her skirt. Joe did not particularly like Sue, but he was nice to her. Bob's cruelty made Joe angry. Miss Hill accused Tom of the prank because the gum wrapper was on his desk. When Bob, sitting in front of Joe, said nothing, Joe poked him and whispered, "C'mon Bob, be a man and take your medicine." That was the push Bob needed to own up to the deed. But the act might have cost Joe the election. As Joe walked into class that morning, he found a paper on his desk that read, "No fink for president." The handwriting was that of Mark, Bob's best friend. Joe crumpled the paper and threw it away without even looking at Mark. He started a conversation with Pat.

Later that day, Joe won the election by a landslide. As everyone was congratulating him, Mark extended his hand and said, "Sorry about that note. I was just so mad that Bob got in trouble." "Forget it," said Joe. "We all have to work together."

CHRISTIAN LOVE

Loving like Jesus means having hearts big enough for all people—our families, our friends, our parish community, and our brothers and sisters in other countries. We are to show the warmth, love, and acceptance of Jesus Christ to the poor, the sick, strangers, and even those who have hurt us. Jesus appreciated the response of love he found in people. He praised positive attitudes, generosity, and service.

Can you recognize love? Read the Gospel verses. Underline the response of love people gave.

1. Mary, the sister of Martha (Luke 10:38–42)

   kindness   listening   serving

2. Martha (Luke 10:38–42)

   serving   healing   listening

3. Samaritan leper (Luke 17:11–19)

   generosity   preaching   expressing thanks

4. Nobleman (Luke 7:1–10)

   teaching   faith   patience

5. Andrew (John 1:40–42)

   joy   leading friends to Christ   singing

6. Joseph of Arimathea (Matthew 27:57–60)

   peace   sharing possessions   mercy

7. Women who followed Jesus (Luke 8:1–3)

   hospitality   trust   patience

What response of love does Jesus ask from Peter (Matthew 18:21–22)?

_____

_____

What response of love have you witnessed recently?

_____

_____

_____

_____

CHRISTIAN SERVICE

At baptism we received the virtue of love. This supernatural power enables us to love and serve others without counting the cost, to see Christ in them, and to avoid hurting them. It makes us eager to reach out to others with concern. It leads us to use our gifts and talents to meet their needs. Confirmation makes our love grow.

We show we have loving hearts when we perform the **works of mercy.** As members of the Christian community, we are actively concerned about those who do not have enough clothes or food or a good home. We meet their physical needs through the **corporal works of mercy.** We also want to help those who are hurt, discouraged, sick, or old. We meet the social, emotional, and spiritual needs of people through the **spiritual works of mercy.** The Spirit helps us know what to do.

WORKS OF MERCY

Here are ways the Spirit leads us to carry out the works of mercy. Check the ones you perform.

Corporal Works

Feed the hungry; give drink to the thirsty
- ❏ I share food and money with the needy.
- ❏ I give part of my lunch to someone who does not have a lunch.
- ❏ I do not waste food or drink.

Clothe the naked
- ❏ I give useful clothing to the poor.
- ❏ I mend old garments for the poor.
- ❏ I take care of the things I own.
- ❏ I generously share my clothing with my brothers and sisters.

Visit the sick
- ❏ I visit the sick and encourage them.
- ❏ I write or call elderly relatives and friends.

Shelter the homeless
- ❏ I support homes for children, the elderly, and the mentally retarded.
- ❏ I welcome newcomers.
- ❏ I treat homes and yards with respect.

Visit the imprisoned
- ❏ Under the guidance of an adult, I write to prisoners.
- ❏ I pray for those who have done wrong and for those assigned to help them.

Bury the dead
- ❏ I attend wakes and funerals.
- ❏ I write letters to those who have lost a loved one.

Spiritual Works

Warn the sinner
- ❏ I show a good example to others.
- ❏ I show displeasure when wrong is done.
- ❏ I support those who are doing right.
- ❏ I give good advice to my friends who may be tempted to do wrong.

Instruct the ignorant
- ❏ I teach my brothers and sisters the faith.
- ❏ I teach prayers to younger children.

- ❏ I remind my friends to be faithful in going to church.
- ❏ I bring a friend to religion class.
- ❏ I read good books about the faith. I share what I have read.
- ❏ I encourage my family to participate in Sunday Mass.
- ❏ I help my brothers and sisters to see that fighting is not Christlike.

Counsel the doubtful
- ❏ I am ready to explain my faith to those who are unsure.
- ❏ I participate in religion class in order to help others.
- ❏ I join in singing and praying at Mass, even if my friends don't.

Comfort the sorrowing
- ❏ I encourage those who are discouraged by difficulties and trials.
- ❏ I spend time with those who are sad and cheer them up.
- ❏ I greet others when I meet them.

Bear wrongs patiently
- ❏ I do not seek revenge.
- ❏ I try not to complain about what others have said and done to me.
- ❏ I avoid anger and cultivate self-control and meekness.

Forgive all injuries
- ❏ I never hold grudges.
- ❏ I forgive someone who has hurt me. I show forgiveness by words and actions.
- ❏ I do not bring up past hurts over and over again.

Pray for the living and the dead
- ❏ I pray, especially during Mass, for my family, friends, and those who have died.
- ❏ I do not let a day go by without remembering others in prayer.
- ❏ I pray especially for those I do not like and who have hurt me in any way.

Write an example of how Jesus performed a corporal work of mercy.

An example of how Jesus performed a corporal work of mercy. is by visiting the sick.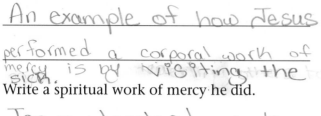

Write a spiritual work of mercy he did.

Jesus teached people to pray.

How have people in your country helped people in another country recently?

_____

_____

JUSTICE
A basic way to love and serve people is to protect their rights. Every person in the world has the right to food, clothing, shelter, and a just wage. Every person has the right to life and to freedom. Sometimes we work for justice by

giving people what they need. But sometimes justice means speaking up for people, teaching them, and standing with them. Justice is a matter of love.

Name a group who is in need of justice.

_____

What can you do to help them?

_____

_____

SECRET SERVICE
Your attitudes toward service can teach people how to have a heart for others. Think about it! Is your attitude toward service positive? Do you look for ways to serve others? Do you serve others with love and joy? Do you consider it a privilege to serve? Followers of Christ who believe in their hearts that Christ loves them will show that same love to others.

There is no limit to the amount of love we may show or the service we may give. We must make sure that we do all acts of mercy for love of God and not for the praise or thanks we may receive. Even if we are never thanked, even if no one ever finds out about all the good we have done, God knows. And our good deeds make us more Christlike.

When we reach out to others in service with the joy and strength of the Holy Spirit, we find we are the ones who really receive. We receive Christ, who lives in the people we serve.

Nominations for Greatness!
The secret of greatness is given in Mark 10:43. What does Jesus say it is?

_____

A great person has a heart for others. Whom would you nominate for the kind of greatness Jesus describes?

_____

SAINTS OF MERCY

Write the work of mercy that BEST fits each saint.

Rose of Lima's mother wanted her to marry a rich man. Instead Rose became a Third Order Dominican, who lived at home and prayed.

1. _____

John Bosco believed young people develop character and virtue in an atmosphere of love. He took boys from the streets and taught them to know God and to practice a skill.

2. _____

John Chrysostom was named "golden-tongued" for his preaching. In 397, people were tempted to doubt their faith and believe heresies. John guided them to have faith.

3. _____

Martin de Porres, the son of a black freed woman and a Spanish nobleman, cared for the sick and the poor. He forgave those who mistreated him because of his race.

4. _____

Although Frances of Rome was the wife of a nobleman and a devoted mother, she went to the hospital every day to nurse the sick. During a plague she turned part of her house into a hospital. God gave her the gift of healing.

5. _____

Margaret of Scotland cared for the poor. She washed their feet and served them herself. Margaret made sure they had food and drink.

6. _____

7. _____

Vincent de Paul wrote more than three thousand letters. He counseled people to forget their own sorrows and to think of others.

8. _____

Louise de Marillac was a friend of Vincent de Paul. She formed the Daughters of Charity in the seventeenth century. They went into hospitals and cared for the sick. They also gave the poorest who died a decent burial.

9. _____

Francis of Assisi was disowned by his family when he began to help the poor. Francis offered up this wrong and continued to practice charity.

10. _____

Before becoming a bishop, Martin of Tours was a soldier. One winter night he saw a shivering beggar at the city gate. Martin cut his own cloak in two and gave one half to the man.

11. _____

Peter Claver saw the misery of slaves. He dedicated his life to caring for these imprisoned people. He would run to ports with medicine and food when the slave ships arrived.

12. _____

Pope Gregory the Great led the Church when barbarians overran Europe. He encouraged monasteries to open their doors to those who had lost their land.

13. _____

Elizabeth of Portugal was a peacemaker. She reconciled her husband and relatives as well as warring kings. Once she even stood on a battlefield and pleaded for peace.

14. _____

FOR CONFIRMATION

Service Projects

Keep a record of the service you do during your time of preparation for Confirmation. Write about it in your journal regularly. After you have reached out to others in Christian service, reflect on your experience. You might complete the following statements in your journal.

- ✦ I tried to show Christlike love and service by . . .

- ✦ I chose to do this because . . .

- ✦ The virtues that the Holy Spirit helped me strengthen in myself by doing this service are . . .

- ✦ The gift of the Holy Spirit that helped me most was . . .

- ✦ By doing this service, I learned that Christian service means . . .

- ✦ Doing this project helped me appreciate . . .

- ✦ Two important events that happened to me while doing this project were . . .

- ✦ These people taught me . . .

- ✦ I saw Christ most in . . .

- ✦ This project will help me later in life because it taught me . . .

- ✦ I can follow up this project by . . .

Celebration: Blessings of the Candidates

Song

Reader: John 13:12–15
Celebrant: Lord Jesus Christ,
  when you climbed the mountain to preach,
  you turned your disciples from the paths of sin
  and revealed to them the beatitudes of your kingdom.
  Help these your servants, who hear the word of the Gospel,
  and protect them from the spirit of greed, of lust, and of pride.
  May they find the blessings of your kingdom
  in poverty and in hunger,
  in mercy and in purity of heart.
  May they work for peace and joyfully endure persecution
  and so come to share your kingdom
  and experience the mercy you promised.
  May they finally see God in the joy of heaven
  where you live and reign for ever and ever.

All: Amen.

(Celebrant, with arms extended, blesses the candidates.)
Celebrant: Lord,
  look with love on your servants,
  who commit themselves to your name
  and bow before you in worship.
  Help them to accomplish what is good;
  arouse their hearts,
  that they may always remember your works and your commands
  and eagerly embrace all that is yours.
  Grant this through Christ our Lord.

All: Amen.

What are Beatitudes?
Beatitudes are Jesus' guidelines for Christlike living. Each one includes an attitude and the promise of happiness in God's kingdom.

What is Jesus' new commandment?

> Love one another. As I have loved you, so you also should love one another. This is how all will know that you are my disciples, if you have love for one another.
> John 13:34–35

Words to Know

- Beatitudes
- justice
- works of mercy

Words to Memorize

Beatitudes   works of mercy

RESPOND

Choose a Beatitude to emphasize during your preparation for Confirmation. In your journal write a prayer asking the Holy Spirit to help you to be and to do what this Beatitude requires. Then list three specific ways you can practice it.

REACH OUT

1. Neatly letter the Beatitudes on white drawing paper. Decorate around them. Paste the sheet in your journal or put it where you will see it at home.
2. Read a biography of St. Vincent de Paul or another Christian known for service.
3. Try to give Christian service at home.
   - Do what you are told immediately.
   - Cooperate with family projects.
   - Share with your brothers and sisters.
   - Volunteer to do more than you have to, when helping around the house.
   - Pray for your family.
4. Evaluate your love life. For each response of love, rate yourself 1 (never), 2 (sometimes), or 3 (all the time). Write a resolution to improve in your weakest point.

2	Listening
___	Leading friends to Christ
3	Serving
3	Forgiveness
3	Expressing thanks
2	Sharing possessions
___	Faith
___	Hospitality

5. Find a way to support the missions.
6. Take a stand for justice on some current issue by making a phone call or writing a letter to someone who can take action.

REVIEW

Keys to Happiness   In the second column write one way you can live each Beatitude right now.

BEATITUDE ATTITUDE	PRACTICE
Be poor in spirit	
Be meek	
Mourn	Pray for people.
Hunger and thirst for right	
Be merciful	
Be clean of heart	Go confess.
Be peacemakers	Avoid violence and try to stop it.
Be persecuted for the sake of righteousness	

The Truth about Love   Write **+** if the statement is true and **O** if it is false.

_O_   1. Jesus replaced the Ten Commandments with a new one.
_+_   2. Christians are to love everyone, even those who hate them.
_+_   3. Jesus wants us to love others as much as he loves us.
_+_   4. Baptism and Confirmation give us a virtue that helps us to love.
_O_   5. The works of mercy are special acts of love to be performed only by priests and religious.
_O_   6. The corporal works of mercy meet emotional and spiritual needs.
_+_   7. Justice is a way of loving people by protecting their rights.
_+_   8. In God's eyes the greatest people are the servants of all.

Spotting the Needy   Write the work of mercy that would meet the needs of these people:

1. Sam has been in jail for six months for stealing from a shop.

Visit the imprisoned.

2. The Thom family, who are refugees from Cambodia, do not know English.

Instruct the ignorant

3. Sally, a bag lady, wanders the streets.

Shelter the homeless.

4. Lisa is upset because her mom and dad are getting a divorce.

Comfort the sorrowing.

5. John apologizes for ruining your art project.

Forgive all injuries.

6. The man repairing your roof on a hot day asks for something to drink.

Give drink to the thirsty.

7. Lou asks you to pray that he does well on an important exam.

Pray for the living and dead.

8. Your grandmother is in the hospital.

Visit the sick

9. Your friend asks what you would do if you were in his shoes.

Counsel the doubtful

10. People are starving to death in Africa.

Feed the hungry.

11. A classmate who doesn't like you is trying to ruin your reputation.

Bear wrongs patiently.

12. Your friend's father is killed in an accident.

Bury the dead

13. The children of a neighbor seldom have new clothes.

Clothe the naked.

14. Your younger sister lies to your parents.

Instruct the ignorant

5 Confirmed in Holiness

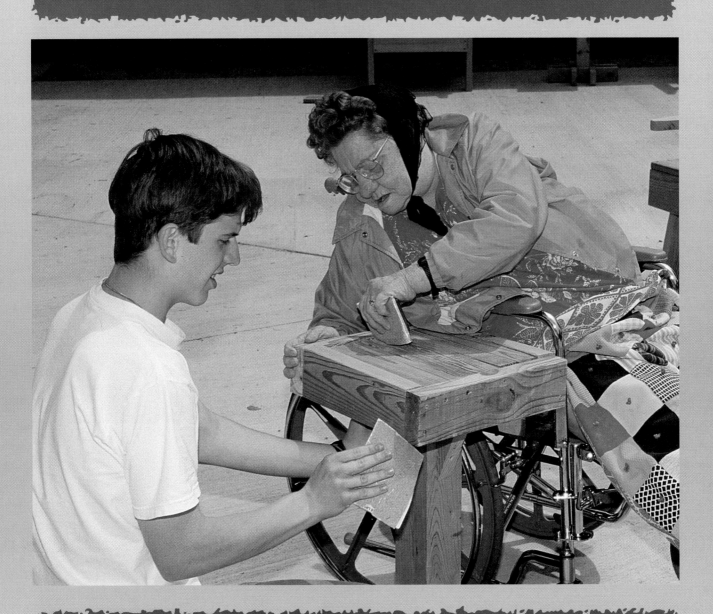

*If we live in the Spirit,
let us also follow the Spirit.*
GALATIANS 5:25

God gave you, your family, and your friends many spiritual gifts at baptism to help you become holy. These gifts are reflected in the way a person responds to various situations. Responses of faith, trust, honesty, prayer, courage, generosity, and kindness are all signs of the spiritual gifts. It is good to be alert to these gifts in others, show we appreciate them, and thank God for them.

Each gift is labeled for a person. Write in each box a spiritual gift evident in that person.

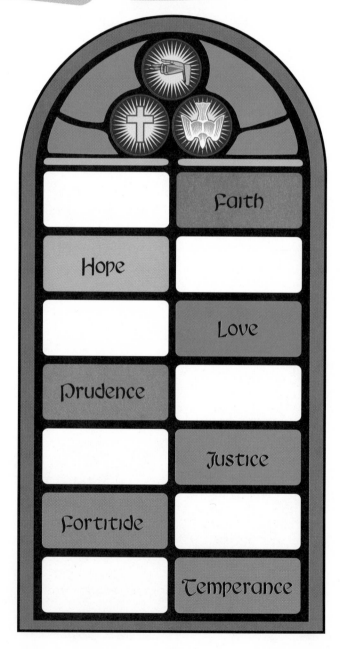

SPIRITUAL BIRTHDAY GIFTS

You received precious gifts from the Spirit when you were born into God's family. All of them are strengthened in you at confirmation.

The **theological virtues** help you direct your life toward God:

 Faith is the power to trust God completely and accept as true all God has revealed and teaches through the Catholic Church.

Hope is the power to trust that God will give you eternal life and all the help necessary along the way.

Love (charity) is the power that enables you to love God, to give God first place in your life, and to love others for love of God.

The **cardinal moral virtues** help you to act the right way:

 Prudence empowers you to decide what is good or best and choose it.

Justice empowers you to respect others' rights and give them their due.

Fortitude gives you the courage to do what is right even when it is very difficult.

Temperance empowers you to control your desire for pleasure.

Think of a symbol for each virtue. Draw it in the pane next to its name on the stained-glass window.

Along with the theological and cardinal virtues, at baptism the Holy Spirit poured special gifts upon you—seven supernatural habits. These marvelous **gifts of the Spirit** are with you now. In confirmation there will be a fuller outpouring of these gifts to help you persevere in your friendship with God and live an active Christian life. In critical situations, when you find it hard to cope with problems or to make decisions, these gifts guide you. They enable you to respond to God promptly and lovingly.

The prophet Isaiah proclaimed the coming of the Messiah.

The Spirit of God would be with him, and he would possess all the great virtues of his ancestors: the wisdom of Solomon, the courage of David, the knowledge of God that Abraham and Moses had. Isaiah 11:2–3 lists the gifts of the Spirit. Read Luke 4:18–19 to see what Jesus was to do with his gifts.

The first four gifts help us to *know* God's will. The other three help us to *do* God's will. Read about each gift of the Spirit in the next sections. The question will help you reflect on how the Spirit is at work in your heart already.

KNOW GOD'S WILL	DO GOD'S WILL
Wisdom Understanding Right Judgment Knowledge	Courage Reverence Wonder and Awe

This book refers to the gifts by the names used in the new Rite of Confirmation. The traditional names are in parentheses.

WISDOM

Some people believe in life after death. Others think we had better enjoy the pleasures of this life to the hilt because that's all there is. Some people see abortion and capital punishment as evils. Others don't. Some people think the Mass is a waste of time. Others celebrate the Eucharist daily because to them it is the greatest thing they can do. How do you know what's true?

Wisdom enables you to love the things of God. It helps you to see life from God's point of view. You recognize the real value of persons, events, and things. Wisdom keeps you from foolishly judging only by appearances. It makes you mature in the way you think and act.

Right now wisdom makes you appreciate the Sacrament of Confirmation. It leads you to work toward being confirmed not because your parents expect it, or because everyone else your age is doing it, but because you see its value and desire it.

Read Colossians 1:9–10. What manner of life will wisdom enable you to lead?

_____

Read Matthew 7:24–27. What does Jesus say a wise person does?

_____

When did you make a wise decision?

_____

UNDERSTANDING

Persons blind from birth know that the sky is blue and the grass is green, but they don't know what color *means*. Similarly, you can recite the truths of the Catholic Church and not really know what they mean. How do you come to realize the beauty and significance of our faith?

Understanding gives you insight into the truths of faith. You know the meaning and the consequences of what God tells you about himself and all of creation. Understanding grows through prayer and the reading of Scripture.

Right now understanding enables you to realize the impact Confirmation ought to make on your life. You comprehend the gifts it will bring to you as well as the responsibilities it will entail.

Read Mark 4:35–41. What didn't the apostles understand yet?

_____

_____

How does understanding that Jesus is God affect your life?

_____

_____

_____

RIGHT JUDGMENT (Counsel)

How often have you lost sleep and gotten headaches from agonizing over a decision? You feel responsible, confused, and alone. How do you know what is the right thing to do?

> The gift of right judgment helps you to *seek* advice and to be open to the advice of others. Using this gift, you seek direction in the Sacrament of Reconciliation and you ask advice from a parent or friend. Right judgment also helps you to *give* advice. It enables you to help others with their problems: to speak up and encourage them to do the right thing.

Right now, through the gift of right judgment, you are determining if you are ready to be confirmed. You are consulting your parents, priest, catechist, and others for help in taking this next step in your spiritual journey.

Read the counsel (advice) Jesus gives in Luke 6:27–35. Write your favorite part.

_____

Write about a time when you were glad you followed someone else's advice.

_____

_____

_____

KNOWLEDGE

If you wish to live well, you have to know what life is all about. You have to know the teachings of Jesus. How do you become open to what God and life have to teach you?

> The gift of knowledge helps you realize the truths of the universe. You experience God. You come to know who you are and the true value of things through life events. This gift also enables you to recognize temptations for what they are and turn to God for help.

Right now the gift of knowledge is at work in you as you evaluate your experience of the Christian life. What you know of Jesus and his example and what you know of the Church—its worship, its faith, and its service—will help you commit yourself to Christ and the Church as a confirmed Christian.

What can you know with the gift of knowledge? Read Ephesians 1:17–19 to find out.

_____

_____

Tell about a time you learned something about God's love for you.

_____

_____

COURAGE (Fortitude)

Christians today are challenged to take stands that are unpopular. The use of drugs and alcohol is commonplace. Indulging in sex outside marriage and keeping quiet about injustices are part of the world scene. It isn't easy to be different. How do you get the strength to live by the principles and values of Jesus?

The gift of courage enables you to stand up for your beliefs and to live as a follower of Christ. With this gift you have the inner strength to do what is right in the face of difficulties and to endure suffering with faith. Courage helps you to undertake challenging tasks in the service of God. But it also takes courage to be faithful just to ordinary duties. It takes strength to live a good Christian life when no one praises you or notices your efforts.

Right now it takes courage to devote yourself to preparing for Confirmation. It's hard to go to class when your friends don't or when there's an exciting activity at the same time. It's difficult to try to change your habits to become a better Christian. It's a challenge to improve your prayer life, to participate in the Eucharist and Reconciliation, and to serve others.

List some acts of courage the Ephesian community was to practice. (Ephesians 4:31–32)

_____

_____

_____

Name one ordinary thing you do that takes strength to do well for love of Christ.

_____

Name someone you know who has courage. Explain how it shows.

_____

_____

_____

REVERENCE (Piety)

A girl throws her candy wrapper on the ground. A man shoots a dog just for fun. A gang attacks an innocent bystander. Every day people harm themselves and others. They ruin and destroy things God gave us to enjoy. This would not happen if people had a sense of God's presence in others and in the world. How do you come to be aware of God and respond to God?

Reverence is a gift of the Spirit that helps you love and worship God. Reverence for God leads to prayer (individual and communal) and to a deep respect for God, for all God's people, and for all that God has created.

Right now reverence is enabling you to participate in an act of worship: the Sacrament of Confirmation. It is helping you to strengthen your relationship with God and to increase your love for others and for the world.

Read Ephesians 5:1–5 and 15–20. Write one thing that Paul tells us to do to live as a faithful child of God.

_____

_____

How can you show reverence at this Sunday's Eucharist?

_____

_____

WONDER AND AWE (Fear of the Lord)

Out of respect, Moses removed his sandals when God spoke to him from the burning bush. The Israelites never even dared to pronounce the name of God. We tend to take God for granted, especially since God became "one of us." How anxious we ought to be to please God who is so great and who loves us so very much! How do you come to have the right attitude toward God?

The gift of wonder and awe helps you recognize the majesty of God and your dependence on God. It leads you to marvel at God's great love for you. This gift helps you avoid anything that would separate you from God's love. It helps you to pray and never to lose trust in God.

Right now wonder and awe are increasing your desire to draw closer to God, to do as God wishes, and to become a better person in order to be more worthy to be in God's presence. Out of awe, you will want to celebrate the Sacrament of Reconciliation and make up for the times when you failed to respond to God's great love.

After reflecting on God's mercy, Paul responds with a prayer of praise in Romans 11:33–36. Read it. Write one thing he praises God for.

Write a prayer of thanksgiving praising God for loving you and for your family and friends.

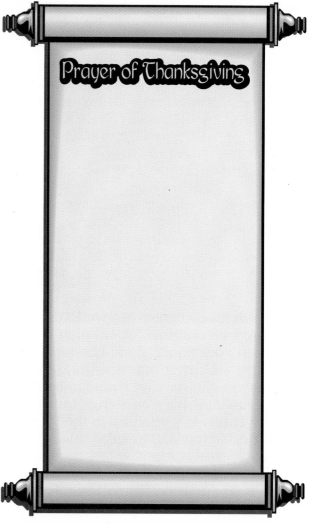

Prayer of Thanksgiving

48

WITNESSES OF THE GIFTS

For each gift, write the name of a person you have seen give witness to this gift. Choose a different person for every gift.

Wisdom: _____

Understanding: _____

Right judgment: _____

Knowledge: _____

Courage: _____

Reverence: _____

Wonder and awe: _____

OTHER GIFTS OF THE SPIRIT

The Holy Spirit gives special gifts called **charisms** or **charismatic gifts** to individual members of the Church. *A charism is a gift given by the Holy Spirit to an individual for the good of others and the Church.* Charisms have been evident in the Church from its beginning. They are given to those whom the Spirit chooses and at any time. These special gifts must be used with the Church's approval for spreading the kingdom of God throughout the world.

Read 1 Corinthians 12:7–11. Unscramble the names of some of the charismatic gifts that are to be used to build up the Body of Christ.

1. legnhai _____

2. yppcreho _____

3. speaking in nougtse _____

4. preaching with smowdi _____

5. ermcails (mighty deeds) _____

6. discernment (recognizing pitssir) _____

7. atihf _____

8. nnttteerriipao of tongues _____

_____

There is one gift that stands out among all the others. It is given to all at baptism for personal holiness and for the growth of the faith community. Find out what this is by reading 1 Corinthians 13:13 and write it here:

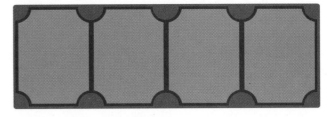

THE SPIRIT IN YOU!

The Holy Spirit inspires you to love God and to serve others. The Spirit dwelling in you leads you to choose to do the right thing, to live the holier way, and to give witness to Jesus. Ask the Holy Spirit to help you pray, to enable you to forgive, and to fill you with enthusiasm for the mission of Christ. Most of all, pray that the Holy Spirit will fill your heart with great love for your faith. Then you will be proud to share it and help build God's kingdom of justice and mercy.

FOR CONFIRMATION

Letter Requesting the Sacrament
Requesting the Sacrament of Confirmation from your bishop or pastor is the official way to express your desire for the sacrament. You may wish to mention in your letter the various ways you have given service.

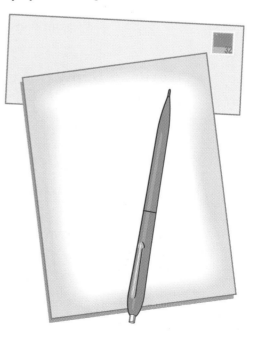

The Spirit gives us good things if we ask. Write a prayer in your journal asking for a particular virtue. Explain why you would like that virtue and what it will empower you to do.

REACH OUT

1. Write your sponsor a note telling about the gifts of the Spirit evident in his or her life.
2. Titus was a young bishop and a friend of St. Paul. Read Titus 3:1–2. What signs of the Spirit does Paul urge Titus to show? Explain in a paragraph how these can help you show loving service.
3. You and your classmates might make banners depicting the seven gifts of the Spirit to display in a suitable place at the time of your confirmation.
4. Find out about the charismatic movement in the Church by doing research and by talking to people.
5. Discuss with your classmates how you can put the gifts into action. For instance, the gift of knowledge can be used by helping in a PSR (CCD) program. Decide on one way you will use a gift.

REMEMBER

What are the gifts of the Spirit?
The gifts of the Spirit are powers given to us at baptism and strengthened at confirmation. They help us persevere in our friendship with God and guide us in our decisions and conduct so that we become more like Jesus.

How is the greatest virtue, love, described in Scripture?

 Love is patient, love is kind. It is not jealous, [love] is not pompous, it is not inflated, it is not rude, it does not seek its own interests, it is not quick-tempered, it does not brood over injury, it does not rejoice over wrongdoing but rejoices with the truth. It bears all things, believes all things, hopes all things, endures all things.

1 Corinthians 13:4–7

Words to Know

+ theological virtues
+ cardinal moral virtues
+ gifts of the Spirit
+ charisms (charismatic gifts)

Words to Memorize

The gifts of the Spirit
(Hint: Think of the acronym "WURK CReW." The gifts are at "work" in us.)

REVIEW

Know Your Gifts   Complete each sentence with the correct answer.

1. At _____, we receive the seven gifts of the Spirit for the first time.

2. The _____ virtues help us direct our lives toward God.

3. The _____ virtues help us act the right way.

4. A _____ is a gift given by the Holy Spirit to an individual for the good of others and the Church.

5. The gift that you most look forward to increasing at your confirmation is

_____

Witnesses of the Gifts In the box name the gift of the Spirit that belongs with the definition.

 The gift of the Spirit that enables us to love the things of God and to see things from God's point of view

 The gift of the Spirit that enables us to know the value of things through our past experience

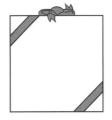 The gift of the Spirit that enables us to love and worship God and respect God's people and all of creation

 The gift of the Spirit that gives us strength to do difficult deeds for love of Christ

 The gift of the Spirit that leads us to seek advice about living a Christian life and enables us to give such advice

 The gift of the Spirit that enables us to have insights into our faith, to see the meaning of what God has told us about himself and creation

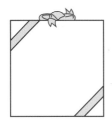 The gift of the Spirit that enables us to recognize the majesty of God and marvel at God's love for us

A Gallery of Gifts Match the name of the gift with its description by writing its letter on the line.

a. fortitude	e. love	h. prophecy
b. hope	f. faith	i. justice
c. prudence	g. healing	j. speaking in
d. temperance		tongues

_____ 1. Theological virtue that helps you trust God completely and accept as true all that God has revealed and teaches through the Catholic Church

_____ 2. Cardinal moral virtue that helps you decide what is good

_____ 3. Theological virtue that empowers you to love God and to give God first place in your life.

_____ 4. The charismatic gift for making other people spiritually or physically well

_____ 5. Cardinal moral virtue that empowers you to respect the rights of others and give them their due

_____ 6. Cardinal moral virtue that gives you the courage to do what is right even when it is very difficult

_____ 7. Theological virtue of trusting that God will give you eternal life and all the help that is necessary along the way

_____ 8. Cardinal moral virtue that empowers you to control your desire for pleasure

_____ 9. Cardinal moral virtue that means the same as one of the seven gifts of the Spirit

_____ 10. The gift that is above all others

Celebration:
Prayer for the Gifts of the Spirit

Leader: We have each received the greatest gift of the Spirit—love. This gift empowers us to serve others in our daily lives.

All: Lord, teach us to love and use all our gifts as you want us to use them.

Leader: Candidates, you are preparing to seal and confirm the gifts of the Spirit you have received at baptism. Are you willing to continue your faith journey in a spirit of generosity and service?

Candidates: We desire to receive the seal of the Holy Spirit at confirmation. May the Spirit renew in us his gifts. May he fill our hearts with courage to make a difference in this world as we witness to our faith.

Reader 1: Pour out your Spirit of wonder and reverence on us that we may be on fire with the love of the Spirit. Let us pray: [Lord, hear our prayer.]

Reader 2: Send your Spirit of wisdom and understanding into the Church to make all who believe one in heart and soul. Let us pray: [Response]

Reader 3: Enlighten our minds with knowledge and right judgment to follow the Gospel of Jesus and the teachings of the Church. Let us pray: [Response]

Reader 4: Through the Spirit of courage, help us serve others and build a world of justice and mercy. Let us pray: [Response]

Song

6 Confirmed in the Church

As a body is one though it has many parts,
and all the parts of the body,
though many, are one body, so also Christ.
For in one Spirit we were all baptized into one body,
whether Jews or Greeks, slaves or free persons,
and we were all given to drink of one Spirit.

1 CORINTHIANS 12:12–13

- A missionary priest stoops to enter a hut in New Guinea to bring Communion to a dying mother.

- Mexican boys and girls clap and sing as they process to church for the feast-day Mass of our Lady of Guadalupe.

- Pope John Paul II canonizes 103 Korean martyrs at a majestic and solemn Mass in Rome.

- One bitter cold night in Russia, a group of refugee prisoners gathers around a stump of a tree which serves as an altar. A priest consecrates the bread and wine that have been smuggled to him.

- The contemplative Benedictine nuns of Stanbrook, England, privately celebrate a jubilee liturgy for a member of their community.

MANY, YET ONE

What makes all of these people one? How are you united with the Church in Korea, England, New Guinea, Mexico, and Russia? When you come together with the Christian community to celebrate the Eucharist, you are united with the Church throughout the world. You are one through Jesus, the Bread of Life. In the Eucharist your bonds with the members of the worldwide Church are strengthened. You show you belong not only to the parish community, but to the universal Church as well.

When you are with your friends, you feel you belong. Every moment is important. You listen intently to what they have to say. You participate in the conversation excitedly. Time goes fast, and you make plans to get together again.

Because of your baptism, you belong to the Body of Christ, the Church, and all the members are your brothers and sisters in Christ. When you participate in the Eucharist, you strengthen your friendship with Jesus, whose love for you is greater than anyone else's. You worship God as God's people and offer together the sacrifice of Calvary, the sacrifice of the Last Supper. *The Eucharist is the center and source of the community of faith.* This sacrament empowers you and others in the Church to love and serve as Jesus did. It does this through the work of the Spirit.

JESUS ALIVE!

The Spirit is always bringing forth Jesus in the world. When the Spirit came to Mary, Jesus came to live in her. When the Spirit came to the apostles, they became Jesus alive in the world. When the Spirit came to you in Baptism, you became another Christ. During the Mass the Spirit speaks through the Scripture. Then at the consecration the priest prays that through the power of the Holy Spirit Jesus becomes present on the altar in the forms of bread and wine. And Jesus is with us.

The Holy Spirit is the Spirit of Jesus bringing you closer to himself. The Holy Spirit makes you one with Jesus and helps you offer yourself with Jesus at the Mass. The Spirit works in the community gathered for the Eucharist and unites all the members in faith and love.

EUCHARIST: THE BREAD AND THE BLESSING CUP

St. Paul knew something was wrong. The people of the Corinthian community were arguing before celebrating the Eucharist. He wrote to them about the Eucharist as the redeeming act of Jesus. Read the Scripture passages and complete the crossword puzzle. Each answer describes what the Church teaches about the Eucharist.

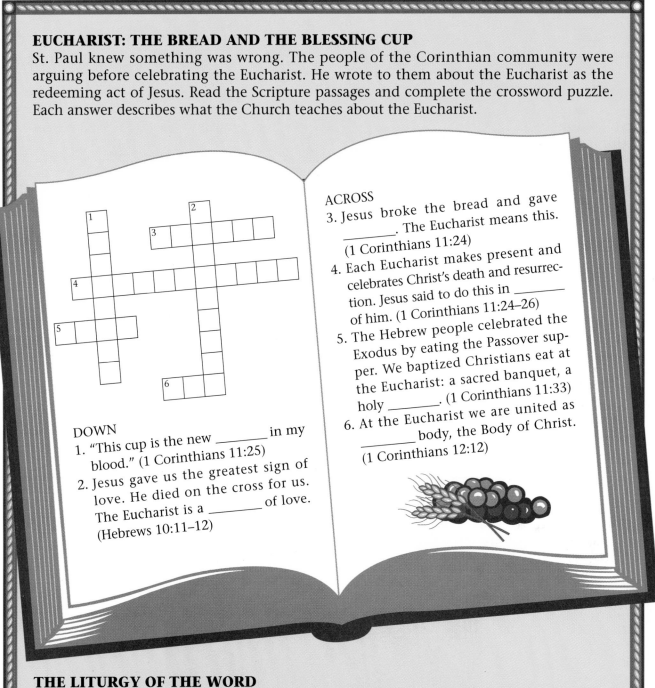

ACROSS

3. Jesus broke the bread and gave _____. The Eucharist means this. (1 Corinthians 11:24)
4. Each Eucharist makes present and celebrates Christ's death and resurrection. Jesus said to do this in _____ of him. (1 Corinthians 11:24–26)
5. The Hebrew people celebrated the Exodus by eating the Passover supper. We baptized Christians eat at the Eucharist: a sacred banquet, a holy _____. (1 Corinthians 11:33)
6. At the Eucharist we are united as _____ body, the Body of Christ. (1 Corinthians 12:12)

DOWN

1. "This cup is the new _____ in my blood." (1 Corinthians 11:25)
2. Jesus gave us the greatest sign of love. He died on the cross for us. The Eucharist is a _____ of love. (Hebrews 10:11–12)

THE LITURGY OF THE WORD

The eucharistic celebration has two main parts: the Liturgy of the Word and the Liturgy of the Eucharist. Both God's Word and Christ's Body and Blood unite us and nourish us as the People of God.

All over the world people hear the Word of God proclaimed at the liturgy. Whether it be in German, English, Swahili, or Russian, it is the same Word uniting us in the one faith to believe in the one God.

Number the parts of the Liturgy of the Word in correct sequence.

_____ Gospel
_____ Responsorial Psalm
_____ Second Reading
_____ Intercessions
_____ Homily
_____ First Reading
_____ Alleluia
_____ Profession of Faith

THE POWER OF GOD'S WORD

If God's Word is to make a difference in your life, you must think about it. Reflect on the following readings often used in the Confirmation liturgy. Note how they unite us in believing, living, and proclaiming God's message.

First Reading: Acts 1:3–8
In this reading God says,

You will receive power when the holy Spirit comes upon you, and you will be my witnesses.

Name two ways the members of your parish community show they are united in giving witness to Jesus.

_____

_____

_____

The **Psalm Response** for this reading is: "You will be my witnesses to all the world." How do you show you are united as Christ's witnesses in prayer at Mass?

_____

_____

_____

_____

Gospel: Luke 4:16–22 (JB)

The Spirit of the Lord has been given to me. He has sent me to bring good news . . . .

◆ How can you bring good news to the sick, the needy, or those who have no friends?

_____

_____

◆ What can you do to show those blind to the needs of others how to love like Jesus?

_____

_____

_____

_____

◆ How can you help those afflicted by unhappy family situations?

_____

_____

_____

THE LITURGY OF THE EUCHARIST

At the Liturgy of the Eucharist, you are united with Jesus and his sacrifice. You receive the Body and Blood of Christ under the forms of bread and wine. When you share in the Eucharist, God unites you to himself and others. You are one with all who belong to the Church on Earth, in heaven, and in purgatory. The Eucharist nourishes you to live out the Word of God you have heard proclaimed.

ONE IN WORSHIP

The Church, the community of believers, prays together. In communal prayer we experience our oneness in giving thanks and praise to God. When we pray as a community Christ's promise is fulfilled:

 Where two or three are gathered together in my name, there am I in the midst of them.   Matthew 18:20

Our common responses express our unity. How readily do you respond in dialogue with the priest at the Eucharist?

Practice the responses to these prayers.
- ✦ Pray, brethren, that our sacrifice may be acceptable to God, the almighty Father.
- ✦ The Lord be with you.
- ✦ Lift up your hearts.
- ✦ Let us give thanks to the Lord our God.
- ✦ Let us proclaim the mystery of faith.
- ✦ This is the Lamb of God, who takes away the sins of the world. Happy are those who are called to his supper.
- ✦ The Body of Christ.

ALL THAT WE HAVE!

People who really care get involved. As fully initiated Christians, we belong to the People of God. We are needed in the Body of Christ. During the Liturgy of the Eucharist, we offer ourselves with and through Christ, in the power of the Holy Spirit, for the praise of the Father. We unite our sacrifices to the sacrifice of Jesus, who makes them pleasing to God. We bring our problems and struggles, our successes and services and offer them to the Father. At Mass we pray for the needs of the Church and the world, and for the coming of the kingdom.

By offering ourselves and praying for needs, we participate in the best way possible. We show how much we trust the power and the goodness of Jesus, who comes to us in Holy Communion. Since the moments spent celebrating Eucharist are the most important ones in your life, respond with the community, pray and sing reverently, and receive Communion.

What will you offer at your next Eucharist?

EVERY MOMENT COUNTS

 Dominic Savio was only fifteen when he died. He was canonized in 1954. Some people wondered, "How did *he* ever become a saint?" Dominic did not work miracles, build schools or hospitals, write books, or found a religious community. In fact he seemed very ordinary.

Dominic was one of ten children born to a blacksmith's family in Italy. At St. John Bosco's school for boys, he joined the usual routine of classes and chores. The only thing the boys noticed about Dominic was his friendliness and cheerfulness. They knew they could count on him to be fair in games, and every boy felt Dominic was his friend.

What they didn't realize was the care Dominic took of his spiritual life. He confided to St. John Bosco that every day he would try to find some way to put into practice the readings he heard at Mass. When Dominic received Communion, he would offer every moment of his day to Christ. How did Dominic Savio become a saint? Through the Eucharist he made every moment of every day count!

1. Why was Dominic's day changed by the Liturgy of the Word?
2. How did Dominic bring the Christ he received in the Eucharist to others? How can *you* bring Christ to others?

WHEN THINGS GO WRONG

As you prepare to become a confirmed Christian, you need to think about the role you play in the community of faith. You are part of a graced community that is united around the Eucharist, giving worship to the Father. But because it is a human community, its members are capable of sin. **Sin** is an action or omission that is contrary to God's law. It is an offense against God and the Church, and it is a failure to love. **Mortal sins** must be confessed in the Sacrament of Reconciliation. These serious sins are committed only when

✓ we have done something that is *seriously wrong*,

✓ we *knew* it was seriously wrong, and

✓ we *freely and willingly chose* to do it.

Venial sins are lesser sins. They can be forgiven by prayer, good actions, and receiving the Eucharist. But it is recommended that you confess them in the Sacrament of Penance, too.

Just as the goodness of all in the community strengthens the Body of Christ, so the sins of all hurt and weaken it. They bring division. Sin causes us to be at odds with ourselves, others, and God. When we are wounded by sin, Christ heals us through the Sacrament of Reconciliation. He came to gather what was scattered, to heal the brokenhearted, and to restore what was lost by sin. Christ challenges us to forgive one another as he forgives us, and he encourages us to seek forgiveness from him and others. The strength to be healers is given to us by Christ through his Holy Spirit.

———————◆———————

How can we act as healers? Read these stories. Determine who are the healers.

Carla was furious at Lucy for not inviting her to go Christmas caroling with the other girls. To pay Lucy back, Carla made an effort to hurt her by ignoring her. Finally Carla realized that she had overreacted. She felt sorry and asked God's forgiveness. But Carla never showed this sorrow to Lucy. Is Carla a healer? Why or why not?

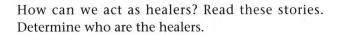

Eric was grounded for a week by his parents because he had lied to them about where he had been. Eric talked the situation over with his parents, apologized, and accepted his punishment. Is Eric a healer? Why or why not?

_____

_____

Bill overheard Steve being corrected by the teacher for stealing. When Bill got to the cafeteria, his classmates wanted to know where Steve was. Bill casually remarked that Steve was busy, and changed the subject. Is Bill a healer? Why or why not?

_____

_____

Beth made fun of Ann in front of her friends by crudely imitating the way Ann sang at practice. Later, Beth came and apologized. Ann told her coldly, "Sorry isn't enough," and walked away. Is Beth a healer? Why or why not?

_____

_____

Is Ann a healer? Why or why not?

_____

Sue's friends, Debbie and Claudia, are angry with each other. Sue listens to both of them but refuses to criticize either girl behind her back. She begs them to talk to each other rather than to her. Is Sue a healer? Why or why not?

_____

_____

CHANGE YOUR HEART

One who stops being better stops being good. Christians are people in a constant state of conversion. The Spirit who comes in Confirmation enables us to change our hearts and become more like Christ. Read the statements and note the ones that do not describe you. Use them to write two resolutions in your journal.

- ✦ If someone hurts me, I look for ways to be extra kind to that person.
- ✦ I celebrate the Sacrament of Penance regularly (at least every month or two).
- ✦ If I hurt someone, I apologize as soon as possible.
- ✦ If someone hurts me, I talk to that person instead of just telling all my friends.
- ✦ If someone apologizes to me, I accept the apology in a friendly manner. I let the person feel as if Christ has forgiven him or her.
- ✦ I refuse to bring up past hurts over and over again.
- ✦ I pray for those I have hurt and those who have hurt me.
- ✦ I make a daily examination of conscience.
- ✦ I go regularly to the same confessor so he can help me.
- ✦ If there are arguments among my friends, I try to act as a peacemaker.
- ✦ If I hurt someone, I don't think up excuses to defend myself.
- ✦ I can admit when I am wrong.

✠ A FORGIVING HEART ✠

The gold candlesticks were layered with wax as the wedding celebration stretched into the night. The guests feasted at the banquet table. Amid the vibrant silks and velvets, there were glimpses of the lovely bride, Jane Frémyot, leading the dancing. Friends commented on how lucky Baron Christophe de Rabutin-Chantal was to have picked such a beautiful bride.

During the next seven happy years, Jane managed the castle. She loved her husband and her four children. She was even like a mother to the servants. Each morning she would gather the household for Mass. During the day, Jane was everywhere—supervising her children's education and singing as she did her work. At her back door, the poor could fill their bowls with soup and receive a piece of bread. She showed her children how to see Christ and love him in others.

Then Jane's warm and secure home was torn with tragedy. Christophe was killed by another man in a hunting accident. "Why did God let this happen?" Jane asked herself. She tried to be positive and forgiving, but it was very hard.

Seven years later she heard the Bishop of Geneva, Francis de Sales, give a spiritual talk. She went to the Sacrament of Reconciliation and told him about her life. Francis led her to see that she must trust God still more and personally forgive the man who had accidentally killed her husband. Jane admitted that she did not have the courage to meet the man or even look at him. But Jane's deep faith helped her to do what was most difficult: to forgive the one who hurt her most. Eventually she became a godparent for this man's child. At last she felt the peace of Christ that comes from a forgiving heart.

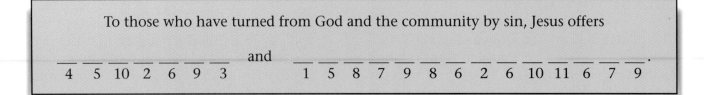

To those who have turned from God and the community by sin, Jesus offers

__ __ __ __ __ __ __ and __ __ __ __ __ __ __ __ __ __ __ __ .
4   5   10   2   6   9   3   1   5   8   7   9   8   6   2   6   10   11   6   7   9

THE SACRAMENT OF RECONCILIATION

In the Sacrament of Reconciliation, or Penance, we encounter Jesus and ask him to forgive us through the priest, the ordained minister of his Church. We trust in God's mercy and in the forgiveness of others who belong to the community of faith. Through the priest, who represents Jesus and the forgiving community, we are absolved from our sins and reconciled with God and others. The division caused by our selfishness is healed, and the Christian community is more united. The priest is bound by the seal of confession never to reveal anyone's confession.

As you prepare to celebrate Confirmation, you will want to look for ways to strengthen your relationship with God. Regular celebration of the Sacrament of Penance can help you to foster that growing relationship.

Review the parts of the Sacrament of Reconciliation. Use the terms from the box to identify each part. Then use the numbered letters to complete the sentence at the top of the page.

> ◆ Prayer for light
> ◆ Acts of penance
> ◆ Contrition
> ◆ Examination of conscience
> ◆ Absolution
> ◆ Confession
> ◆ Thanksgiving

1. Asking the Holy Spirit to help you look honestly at yourself

   __ __ __ __ __ __   __ __ __   __ __ __ __
         1   2   3   4

2. Asking yourself questions to see how closely you are following Jesus and his law of love (Reviewing the commandments, the Beatitudes, duties of your state of life, relationships with God, others, and self)

   __ __ __ __ __ __ __ __ __ __ __ __ __

   __ __ __ __ __ __ __ __ __
               5

3. An inner awareness that you have turned from God and hurt others (With a sincere sorrow for sin, this attitude includes the decision to turn from sin and restore love)

   __ __ __ __ __ __ __ __ __
           6

4. Openly acknowledging your faults by telling them to the priest who acts in the name of Christ

   __ __ __ __ __ __ __ __ __ __
             7

5. Prayer, an act of self denial, service, or a work of charity that restores what has been lost or strengthens what has been weakened by sin (satisfaction)

   __ __ __ __   __ __   __ __ __ __ __ __
       8   9

6. God's granting pardon to the sinner by the priest, in the name of Christ, through the ministry of the Church

   __ __ __ __ __ __ __ __ __
   10

7. Spending time in prayer by responding with gratitude to the Father who loves us and reconciles us to himself

   __ __ __ __ __ __ __ __ __ __ __ __
   11

FOR CONFIRMATION

Celebrate the Sacrament of Reconciliation
Although celebrating the Sacrament of Reconciliation before celebrating Confirmation is not required, you may wish to do so. That way you will have everything squared away with the Lord before his Spirit comes to you in a special way. Locate the Reconciliation booklet in the back of this book, tear it out carefully, and fold it. You may wish to use this booklet whenever you go to confession.

REMEMBER

How do the sacraments of Eucharist and Penance unite the Christian community?

In the Eucharist we celebrate the mystery of Jesus' sacrifice of love and the holy meal that gathers us into the Body of Christ. Through the Sacrament of Penance, our sins are forgiven and we are reconciled with God, the community, and ourselves.

Words to Know

- venial sin
- contrition
- mortal sin
- penance
- Eucharist
- absolution
- Liturgy of the Word
- Liturgy of the Eucharist
- reconciliation

Words to Memorize

Act of Contrition

RESPOND

- Read the scripture readings for this week's liturgy. Which has special meaning for you? Your family? Parish? Friends? Why? Record your reflections in your journal.
- *Forgive* is used by Christ over and over. Read and summarize one of these scripture passages. Then write a way you can live it.

Matthew 5:23–24	Luke 15:11–32
Matthew 6:7–15	Luke 23:33–34
Matthew 18:21–22	Luke 23:39–43
Mark 11:25	Luke 24:46–47
Luke 7:36–50	John 20:22–23

REACH OUT

1. Encourage your family to attend a Sunday liturgy together. You may also do this on the anniversary of your First Communion.
2. Find out when the priests or special ministers of the Eucharist bring Communion to the sick. Ask to accompany one of them.
3. Be a peacemaker at school and at home. Keep notes in your journal on what you do to be a Christian who helps and heals.

Celebration: Open to the Spirit

Procession with the Gospel Book

Reading: John 9:1–41 or John 9:1, 6–9, 13–17, 34–38

Leader: Let us bow our heads in silent prayer for the candidates. *(Reflection)*

(If present, sponsors place a hand on the shoulder of their candidates. Candle bearers stand on either side of Leader.)

Leader: Let us pray for the candidates God has called, that they may remain faithful to God, boldly give witness to the words of eternal life, and be a light for the world.

Reader 1: That the Spirit may enlighten their minds and hearts to reject evil and choose good. Let us pray: [Response: Lord, hear our prayer.]

Reader 2: That the Holy Spirit will remove the blindness of selfishness that prevents them from serving you. Let us pray: [Response]

Reader 3: That they may have the faith to recognize Christ in every person they serve. Let us pray: [Response]

Reader 4: That they may overcome the darkness of sin and be strengthened in their weakness. Let us pray: [Response]

(Candidates stand with lighted tapers.)

Leader: Lord Jesus, you are the true light that enlightens the world. By the Spirit of truth, free those who are enslaved by the father of lies. Stir up the desire for good in these candidates whom you have chosen for your sacrament. Let them rejoice in your light, that they may see, and, like the man born blind whose sight you restored, let them prove to be staunch and fearless witnesses to the faith, for you are Lord for ever and ever.

All: Amen.

REVIEW

Eucharist—What Is It? Write words that tell what the Eucharist is on the lines provided. The first letters have been given as clues.

1. M _____

2. L _____

3. S _____

4. S _____

5. R _____

6. P _____

7. C _____

Choose one of the words for Eucharist and explain it.

_____

_____

_____

Sacrament Check Check the true statements.

❏ 1. *Eucharist* means thanksgiving.
❏ 2. The celebration of the Eucharist binds us to Catholics all over the world.
❏ 3. The Eucharist is almost the central event of the community of faith.
❏ 4. In the Eucharist we find strength to love and serve as Jesus did.
❏ 5. Jesus is not actually present in the bread and wine at the Eucharist.
❏ 6. At the Eucharist we offer ourselves with Jesus to the Father.
❏ 7. We hear Scripture proclaimed in the Liturgy of the Eucharist.
❏ 8. You might commit a mortal sin someday without knowing it.
❏ 9. Sin weakens or destroys grace, our relationship with God.
❏ 10. My personal sin does not affect the rest of the Church.

Forgiven and Forgiving For each definition write the letter of the word that matches it best.

a. sin
b. absolution
c. mortal sin
d. contrition
e. penance
f. reconciliation
g. confession
h. venial sin
i. priest
j. Jesus
k. Sacrament of Reconciliation
l. Sacrament of Confirmation
m. Church
n. examination of conscience

_____ 1. Making up with someone and becoming friends again
_____ 2. Failing to love; an action or omission that is contrary to God's law
_____ 3. The forgiveness of our sins granted by God
_____ 4. A serious offense against God that is done knowingly and freely
_____ 5. The rite in which sins committed after baptism are forgiven
_____ 6. Acts that make up for our sins
_____ 7. Sorrow for sin with a purpose of not sinning again
_____ 8. Asking yourself questions to see how closely you are following Jesus
_____ 9–10. Two answers that tell who the priest represents as he forgives us our sins
_____

7 Confirmed in Grace

In him you also, who have heard the word of truth,
the gospel of your salvation, and have believed in him,
were sealed with the promised holy Spirit.
EPHESIANS 1:13

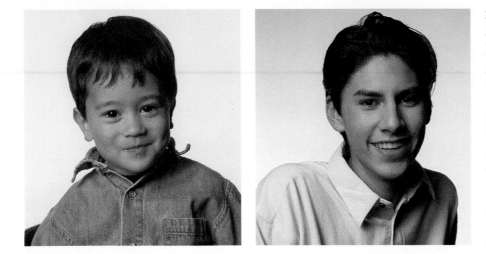

SPIRITUAL GROWTH

Spiritual growth should keep pace with natural growth. At baptism you received grace, divine life. Like Jesus, you have grown in wisdom, age, and grace. You have come to realize God's love for you and what great things God has done for you. You have grown to know and love God. Now you are ready to accept for yourself the privileges and responsibilities of a Christian. You wish to renew your commitment to God, to be anointed by the Spirit, and to share more in the mission of Jesus.

Life has changed much for you because you have grown. You have learned more about the world, you have developed new skills, and you have become more independent.

1. What do you have the ability to do now that you couldn't do when you were three?

   _____

2. With this growth, you have more privileges. What may you do now that you weren't permitted to do when you were younger?

   _____

   _____

   _____

3. You have more responsibilities. As a baby, you were on the receiving end. Nothing much was expected of you. How do you contribute to your family's life now?

   _____

   _____

   _____

4. Looking into the future, what other privileges and responsibilities will you have to handle as you grow older?

   _____

   _____

   _____

CONFIRMATION

Confirmation celebrates the gift of the Spirit. In this sacrament you are endowed by the Spirit with special strength to live God's life more fully, imitate Christ more closely, and witness to our faith and Christ more courageously. You are bound more closely to the Church, and the whole community celebrates with you your commitment to Jesus and his Church. It prays that the Spirit will bless you with the graces you need to grow in Christ.

Ideally Confirmation is celebrated during the *Eucharist*. This expresses more clearly the unity of the sacraments of initiation. Christian initiation is completed by participation in the communion of the Body and Blood of Jesus. If your confirmation is not within the Mass, the rite still includes prayer, readings, intercessions, the Our Father, and blessings.

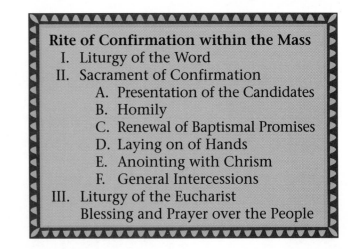

Rite of Confirmation within the Mass
I. Liturgy of the Word
II. Sacrament of Confirmation
   A. Presentation of the Candidates
   B. Homily
   C. Renewal of Baptismal Promises
   D. Laying on of Hands
   E. Anointing with Chrism
   F. General Intercessions
III. Liturgy of the Eucharist
   Blessing and Prayer over the People

THE BEGINNING

The opening prayer for the Rite of Confirmation is one of the following four. Underline the words in each that tell why we ask the Father to send the Spirit.

Put a star by the prayer you would prefer for your confirmation.

_____ 1. God of power and mercy, send your Holy Spirit to live in our hearts and make us temples of his glory.

_____ 2. Lord, fulfill your promise: Send your Holy Spirit to make us witnesses before the world to the Good News proclaimed by Jesus Christ, our Lord.

_____ 3. Lord, send us your Holy Spirit to help us walk in unity of faith and grow in the strength of his love to the full stature of Christ.

_____ 4. Lord, fulfill the promise given by your Son and send the Holy Spirit to enlighten our minds and lead us to all truth.

CELEBRATION OF THE WORD

The Word of God brings the Holy Spirit to us. In it, we find God's will for us. Some suggested readings for Confirmation are listed here. You might be able to choose one from each set for your ceremony. Circle your choices and write a summary statement on the lines provided.

First Reading: Isaiah 11:1–4a
Isaiah 61:1–3a, 6a, 8b–9
Ezekiel 36:24–28

_____

_____

_____

Second Reading: Acts 1:3–8
Acts 2:1–6, 14, 22b–23, 32–33
Romans 8:14–17

_____

_____

_____

PRESENTATION OF THE CANDIDATES

After the readings, the ministers are seated and the candidates are presented for Confirmation. You are called by name or as a group. You enter the sanctuary with your parents or sponsor, or you simply stand in your place. This shows that you desire to declare yourself a Christian and are willing to live like one. Then the bishop gives a homily to explain the meaning of Confirmation.

RENEWAL OF PROMISES

At the end of the homily you stand and renew your commitment to Christ. You publicly renew your baptismal promises. The bishop asks, *"Do you reject Satan and all his works and all his empty promises?"* You respond, *"I do."* Then, by asking the questions boxed in Chapter 3 of this book, he asks you if you believe the faith of the Church. You answer, *"I do."*

Write one special promise you will make on your confirmation day.

_____

_____

_____

After your profession of faith, the bishop invites everyone to pray with him for the Holy Spirit to come to you. He says:

> My dear friends: in baptism God our Father gave the new birth of eternal life to his chosen sons and daughters. Let us pray to our Father that he will pour out the Holy Spirit to strengthen his sons and daughters with his gifts and anoint them to be more like Christ the Son of God.

Underline the two things that the Spirit will do, according to this prayer.

The laying on of hands, or imposition, is a solemn gesture the apostles used as a sign that they were bringing down the power of God. To invoke the Holy Spirit, the bishop and any priests who will administer the sacrament with him extend their hands over the candidates. This is a **general imposition,** not the imposition that actually confirms you.

At this point in the ceremony, the bishop, your parents and sponsors, the congregation, and you are all united in focusing on the one thought:

The bishop prays:

> All-powerful God, father of our Lord Jesus Christ,
> by water and the Holy Spirit
> you freed your sons and daughters from sin
> and gave them new life.
> Send your Holy Spirit upon them
> to be their Helper and Guide.
> Give them the spirit of wisdom and understanding,
> the spirit of right judgment and courage,
> the spirit of knowledge and reverence.
> Fill them with the spirit of wonder and awe in your presence.
> We ask this through Christ our Lord.

Underline the prayer's reference to your baptism.

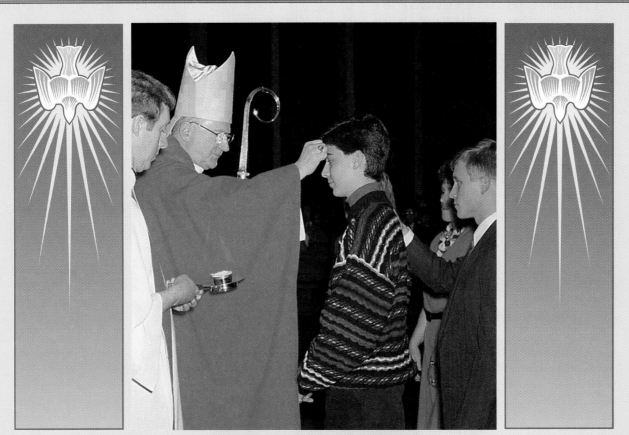

Confirmed in the Spirit

The climax of the Confirmation rite occurs when the bishop lays his hand on your head and anoints you. You come before him with your sponsor. Your sponsor places his or her hand on your right shoulder.

- ✦ Either you or your sponsor presents your confirmation name to the bishop.
- ✦ The bishop traces the sign of the cross with chrism on your forehead and says the words, *"[Name], be sealed with the Gift of the Holy Spirit."*
- ✦ You respond, *"Amen."*
- ✦ Then the bishop extends to you a sign of peace. He might clasp your hand and say, *"Peace be with you."*
- ✦ You answer, *"And also with you."*

With the bishop's anointing, you receive the indelible character, the seal of the Lord, and the gift of the Spirit. You become more like Christ and receive the grace to spread the Lord's presence. You are fully commissioned to be his witness.

As you are confirmed by the bishop for service and discipleship, what might you say to the Holy Spirit?

_____

_____

THE LITURGY OF THE EUCHARIST

The eucharistic liturgy continues with intercessions offered for the whole Church. What intentions would you like to include on your confirmation day?

_____

_____

_____

In the Liturgy of the Eucharist, you and the other newly confirmed, who have been united in the gift of the Spirit, are bound together in the worship of the Father through his Son Jesus Christ. You are joined more closely with one another in praying the Our Father, in sharing the sign of Christ's peace, and in receiving Communion. When you participate in the Eucharist, you celebrate most fully the life of faith that has been confirmed in you through the action of the Holy Spirit.

BLESSINGS

The Eucharist ends with a solemn blessing or prayer over the people for the entire assembly of Christians. The bishop extends his hands over all and uses one of the following:

God our Father
made you his children by water and the
　Holy Spirit:
may he bless you
and watch over you with his fatherly love.
R. Amen
Jesus Christ the Son of God
promised that the Spirit of truth
will be with his Church forever:
may he bless you and give you courage
in professing the true faith.
R. Amen
The Holy Spirit
came down upon the disciples
and set their hearts on fire with love:
may he bless you,
keep you in faith and love,
and bring you to the joy of God's kingdom.
R. Amen.
May almighty God bless you,
the Father, and the Son, ✝ and the Holy Spirit.
R. Amen.

God our Father,
complete the work you have begun
and keep the gifts of your Holy Spirit
active in the hearts of your people.
Make them ready to live his Gospel
and eager to do his will.
May they never be ashamed
to proclaim to all the world Christ crucified
living and reigning for ever and ever.
R. Amen.
And may the blessing of almighty God
the Father, and the Son, ✝ and the Holy Spirit,
come upon you and remain with you forever.
R. Amen.

In the first blessing, underline the ways each Person of the Trinity will bless you. In the second prayer, find three things the Father will enable you to do through the Spirit. Write them:

To _____

To _____

To _____

GROWTH IN CHRIST

To grow spiritually is to become more like Christ. St. Paul said he would feed people solid food, not milk, if they were spiritual adults instead of infants in Christ.

Read St. Paul's definition of a spiritually mature person in 1 Corinthians 2:15–16.

What can a spiritual person judge?

_____

What does he or she have?

_____

Read Romans 8:28–30. Who intends for us to become true images of Jesus?

_____

Read Romans 8:17. What does being a co-heir with Christ involve?

_____

How can being like Jesus bring suffering?

_____

_____

_____

Portrait of a Christian

Decide if each action is something a Christian would do. If it is, shade in the triangles marked with the corresponding number. If your answers are correct, you will see a portrait of a Christian.

1. Share what you have with others.
2. Be patient with the faults of others.
3. Let other people know how great you are.
4. Make as much money for yourself as you can.
5. Be mindful of God every day.
6. Be kind to those who are mean to you.
7. Offer your sufferings for a good intention.
8. Go along with the crowd even if they do wrong, just as long as you belong.
9. Forgive those who hurt you.
10. Say things that will make others feel good about themselves.
11. Guide your friends to do what is right.
12. Don't worry about God and sin until you are old.
13. Tell the truth.
14. Respect those in authority.
15. Tell people off if they offend you.
16. Reach out to those everyone else ignores.
17. Bring others to know and love the Father.
18. Act according to your feelings.

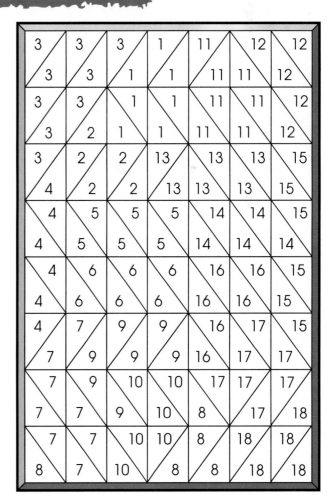

LIVING YOUR COMMITMENT

Anointed, sealed, and blessed in Confirmation, you are ready to bring Christ to the world more effectively. By cooperating with the Holy Spirit, you will grow in the knowledge and love of Jesus. Gradually you will become a true and mature Christian—like Jesus Christ in word and action.

Read these accounts of teenagers striving to live the Christian life. For each one, circle *yes* if you usually do the good action described, or *no* if you usually do not.

1. Every Saturday Annette is driven by her mother to a nursing home. There she helps the residents by writing letters for them, reading to them, or washing their hair.

   yes   no

2. Ellen read that orphans in El Salvador were in need of help. She baby-sat, raked leaves, and did other chores to earn money for them. She sent them $100.

   yes   no

3. A group of boys were picking on a younger boy. Dan went over and got them to stop.

   yes   no

4. On Sunday Judy was in a bad mood. She sulked and then started an argument with her sister, spoiling the day for the rest of the family. In the evening, she apologized to everyone.

   yes   no

5. Ron attends parish activities, such as lectures on the faith and prayer services. Few teens his own age are there.

   yes   no

6. Sara overheard some gossip about Sue. She knew that if she spread it around, Sue's reputation would be ruined, so she kept quiet.

   yes   no

7. Correcting his friend Peter's math test in class, Tim was tempted to overlook some wrong answers so that Peter would pass. He decided to be honest, and he planned to study with Peter for the next test.

   yes   no

8. All weekend Julie was to be busy with her friends. She had only two hours free to help out at home. Then Ann invited her to a movie that was playing during those hours. Julie turned down the invitation.

   yes   no

Now look at one of the accounts you marked *no*. On the lines below, write a Christian way you could respond in a similar circumstance.

_____

_____

A CLOSING THOUGHT

When you are sealed, you are stamped, consecrated, set apart for God. You belong to God, who will use you for his mission. How might God be intending to use you this year to help bring about the kingdom on Earth?

_____

_____

How might God plan to use you in the future?

_____

_____

After Confirmation, how obvious will your seal be? Will people be able to tell from your life that you belong to God?

FOR CONFIRMATION

A Novena
Find the Confirmation Novena in the back of this book. Carefully tear it out and fold it. Use it to prepare for your confirmation.

REMEMBER

How is the Sacrament of Confirmation conferred?
The Sacrament of Confirmation is conferred through the anointing with chrism on the forehead that is done by the laying on of the hand and with the words, "[*Name*], be sealed with the Gift of the Holy Spirit."

RESPOND

Think of one of Jesus' virtues that you admire. Consider how you can grow in this virtue and, in your journal, write a three-point strategy. Then write a short prayer to the Holy Spirit, asking for help to become another Christ.

REACH OUT

1. Read a biography of a Christian known for his or her faith.
2. Invite a friend to your confirmation (perhaps a non-Catholic friend). Explain to this person what Confirmation is all about.
3. Plan a reception with your class to be held immediately after confirmation. Invite your parents, sponsors, catechists, priests, the bishop, and friends. Prepare thank-you cards, decorations, and refreshments with a Spirit theme.
4. Ask a priest what his anointing at Holy Orders meant to him.
5. Write a paragraph on one of the following topics:
   Confirmation Is a New Beginning
   My Faith Is Important to Me
   My Faith Needs to Grow
   Confirmation Empowers Me

Steps to the Spirit   Number the steps of the Rite of Confirmation in the order they occur.

_____ Liturgy of the Eucharist

_____ Anointing with chrism

_____ Homily

_____ Liturgy of the Word

_____ Laying on of hands

_____ General intercessions

_____ Renewal of baptismal promises

_____ Presentation of the candidates

Why?   Answer the questions.

1. Why is it ideal to celebrate Confirmation during the Eucharist?

   _____

   _____

2. Why does the laying on of hands precede the anointing?

   _____

3. Why is it important to be confirmed?

   _____

   _____

Fill-in   Write the missing words on the blanks.

1. In Confirmation you renew your commitment to Christ by publicly rejecting _____

   and professing to believe _____.

2. The laying on of hands is also called _____.

3. The sign of Confirmation is the anointing with _____.

4. The bishop's words when he confirms are "[*Name*], be _____ with the _____

   of the Holy Spirit."

5. At Confirmation you are sealed with an indelible _____.

6. Through Confirmation the Spirit makes us more and more like _____.

8 Confirmed in Witness

*The fruit of the Spirit is love, joy, peace,
patience, kindness, generosity,
faithfulness, gentleness, self-control.*
GALATIANS 5:22

Your confirmation is a new beginning, a fresh start! Answer these questions:

What was one thing that the bishop told the community at confirmation?

_____

Which part of the confirmation ceremony will you remember most? Why?

_____

How did you celebrate with your family?

_____

Did your parents or sponsor tell you anything about living your faith? Write it here.

_____

How can you tell that the parish community, your family, and your sponsor are very happy and proud you are a confirmed Christian?

_____

READY TO WITNESS!

You are a stronger member of the Christian community. You are ready to be a faithful witness to Jesus and his Church. The Holy Spirit, who filled the early Christians on Pentecost, is with you, empowering you for your mission.

After Confirmation, you may not feel like those early followers of the Way who boldly went out proclaiming the Good News in tongues. You may feel very ordinary. Your growth in the Spirit will be a day-by-day journey.

The time after your confirmation is especially important. You can give witness to the Spirit in your life in many ways. You can join in the Eucharist, pray, perform the works of mercy, and live a courageous Christian life. During this time, the community of faith will continue to support you and encourage you to share your gifts and talents in loving service for Christ.

OPEN TO THE SPIRIT

How open are you to the Spirit's presence in your life? Read each scripture passage. On a sheet of paper list the qualities found in a disciple filled with the Spirit.

Galatians 5:22–24   2 Peter 1:5–7
Ephesians 4:2   Ephesians 4:32

List people who have helped you prepare for Confirmation. Use the virtues you listed to describe how these people have witnessed their love for Christ and the community. What three virtues do you see in your life?

A Plan for Spiritual Growth

These suggestions demand sacrifice and courage. Use them to devise a plan. Resolve to stick to it, starting today!

Eucharist The Eucharist is the most important part of your week.

✦ Prepare to offer yourself with Christ and to receive him in the Eucharist.
✦ Pray at the eucharistic liturgy to love Christ and others more.
✦ After Mass, jot down points from the homily or the readings in your journal.

Prayer Your relationship with God is nurtured through communication.

✦ Each night, read about God's love for you in the Scriptures. Think of how you have loved God.
✦ Write your reflections in your journal.

Works of Charity Jesus showed us what a life of loving service means.

✦ Practice the works of mercy.
✦ Show concern for the poor and needy.
✦ Be of service at home, at school, and in your parish.

Community You share a common vision and love for Christ and other members of his Body, the Church.

✦ Become more involved in your parish.
✦ Know when you need to be reconciled with anyone. Plan a time to participate regularly in the Sacrament of Reconciliation.
✦ Share your faith and grow in it by participating in religion classes.

FRUITS OF THE SPIRIT

Healthy trees flourish and bear fruit: apples, oranges, grapefruits, nuts. If you live united to Christ and follow the guidance of his Spirit, your life will bear the fruit of good works. People will recognize God's presence in you by seeing your good works, your love for others, your service to them. You will be aware of God dwelling within you by the joy you experience in doing good.

There are **twelve fruits of the Holy Spirit.** These are the results of the Spirit's presence and gifts in a believing person. They are also the results of cooperating with God's grace.

Read the descriptions of the fruits of the Spirit and the stories that follow. Find evidence of the fruits of the Spirit in the stories.

 CHARITY Charity is the sign that you love God as your good Father and others as Jesus loves you. Your love is so great that you show selfless service to others by your prayers, words, and actions.

 FAITH (Fidelity) Keep your promises! You are faithful when you show loyalty to God and to other persons to whom you have committed yourself. Faithful people are dependable. They trust and obey always.

If you went into the Berard family's hairdressing shop in Manhattan in the early 1800s, you received much more than a shave and a haircut. Pierre Toussaint, a black slave and a Catholic, worked for the Berard family and was skilled at his trade. Day after day, he listened to people's heartaches and family stories as he did his work. Time after time, he would speak to his customers in simple language about Jesus, Mary, and the importance of loving others. Pierre was never too tired after work to care for the poor. Privately, he sent his money to help boys become priests. Pierre was an ordinary person who showed other ordinary people how to be holy. He was faithful to his baptismal promises. Pierre was not a Catholic only on Sunday; he was one every day of the week.

PRACTICE! Make a list of seven acts of charity a teenager could do.

You must be faithful in the practice of your baptismal responsibilities. How can you show faith?

 **JOY** Joy is deep and constant gladness in the Lord that circumstances cannot destroy. It comes from a good relationship with God and others—a relationship of genuine love.

 **MODESTY** Modesty is moderation in all your actions, especially your conversation and external behavior. Modesty is a sign that you give credit to God for your talents and successes.

Men and women took a second glance at the distinguished and handsome jewel merchant. Few would have guessed that this was Father Edmund Campion, a Jesuit serving undercover in England.

When Queen Elizabeth ascended the English throne (1559), the Catholic Church went underground. The queen forced priests, sisters, and laity to take the Oath of Submission, saying that she ruled the Church and state. Catholics could no longer look to the Holy Father in Rome as their spiritual leader. The practice of the Roman Catholic faith, including Mass, was forbidden. Fearless Jesuit priests dared to enter England in disguise and secretly care for loyal Catholics. Edmund Campion was one of these priests.

Edmund amazed his friends because he was happy even in danger. He enthusiastically went about baptizing, preaching, celebrating Mass, even putting out an underground Catholic newsletter. People praised his outstanding talents, but Edmund Campion always assured them, "It is Christ working in me!" His joy brought new life to Catholics in England. Later, when he was discovered and arrested, Edmund encouraged his fellow Catholic captives on the way to prison. He met death so bravely that other young men who witnessed his death entered the priesthood.

PRACTICE! Read Colossians 1:11–12. Why would Jesus say this to St. Edmund Campion?

Name a talent God has given you. How can you use it to help others?

 BENIGNITY Benignity is a deep kindness that is shown by generous acts of service. Kind people are warm and considerate. They try to see the best in others.

 GOODNESS This fruit of the Spirit flows from God's great love. It is a sign that you love all people without exception and do good to them.

An old woman climbed the last step of the crumbling staircase and leaned against the wall, gasping for breath. Then she knocked. The door opened, and there stood a very refined, red-haired woman in a gray dress.

"Excuse me, ma'am. They said you were a nurse and could help me," said the old lady. "If you can't, they'll send me to die on Blackwell Island."

"Come in," invited Rose Hawthorne.

"I'll pay you when I can," mumbled the woman.

"Nonsense! If you had the money, you could go to a hospital. I help those who can't pay." Rose gently undid the bandage to reveal a cancerous wound on the woman's face. Rose's hand worked quickly to clean the sore.

"You're an awfully kind woman. You must come from a nice family," the old lady said.

Rose stopped and looked at the lady steadily. "I do come from a nice family, God's family. You're part of the family too. And in God's family, we help one another."

Rose Hawthorne did help the poorest and most unloved of God's family. In the 1900s she began caring for the neglected of New York, who were forced to die on Blackwell Island. Soon she received permission to found an order of sisters who cared for incurable cancer patients. These sisters built their home on Rosary Hill in New York.

PRACTICE! Name five people you know, including someone you find difficult to work with. How can you show love for these people this week?

Read 2 Corinthians 9:7. What kind of service does Jesus expect from his followers?

 PEACE Jesus said, "Peace I give to you!" A disciple faithful to God's Will is serene, not overly anxious or upset. Peace comes from knowing that all will work out well because God is with us.

 PATIENCE Life has its daily troubles! Patience is love that is willing to endure life's suffering, delays, and routine. It means not giving up in difficult situations.

"Angelo!" Mama Roncalli wiped her hands on her apron and raised her eyes to heaven. "Dear Lord, what will I do with this boy?"

Angelo sheepishly looked down at his homework paper. "I guess I'm not interested in school right now." He glanced enviously out the window to where his brothers and sisters were playing.

But his mother was not persuaded. "You will finish this paper. Then you can go outside." Reluctantly, Angelo accepted this disappointment and set to work.

Decades later, Angelo, as Pope John XXIII, would have made his mother very proud. He was well-educated and understood God's people. He called the Second Vatican Council to help bring the unity and peace of Christ to the Church and the world. Many of his advisers protested the idea of Church renewal. "It's too big a project! There will be too many problems!" Pope John XXIII accepted their opposition with patience, but he did not give up. He knew that God would guide the Council. Even when Pope John XXIII faced an unfinished Council before he died, he could smile peacefully and say calmly, "God will take care!"

PRACTICE! World peace? Family peace? Inner peace? Which do you see as the greatest need? Write one petition expressing your prayer.

Imagine that you have been asked to write a book called *How to Be Patient* for the spiritual growth of teens. Suggest four ways to practice patience as a Christian youth.

CONTINENCE The self-control that you exercise over bodily desires comes from continence. You can discipline your sexual powers by being modest and respectful of others. With continence you control emotions and desires instead of letting them control you.

CHASTITY Chastity is a deep respect for your sexual powers. It moderates the desire for sexual pleasure according to faith and your state in life.

The face of Ugandan Chief Mwanga twisted in rage. "It can't be true," he yelled to his adviser.

"It is true. Charles Lwanga, your steward, has baptized four more catechumens, all men under the age of twenty-five."

"Don't they fear to die like their friend Joseph Mkasa, who was killed for his disobedience?"

"That's the strange thing," answered the adviser. "They've held even more strongly to their faith after his death. More young men are attracted to Christianity than ever."

The adviser bowed out and left the chief to his gloomy thoughts. The cruel and immoral chief knew what angered him. The Christians refused to engage in homosexual acts with him, and they had reproached him for the murder of an Anglican missionary. The chief's anger overruled his sense of integrity. He ordered the war drums beaten to call the executioners. He didn't know that the blood of martyrs is the seed of the Church.

PRACTICE! The desire for sexual pleasure can get out of control. It can happen to anyone, just as it did to Chief Mwanga. The challenges you meet are as big as the ones the Ugandan martyrs faced. You are challenged to treat others with respect in your words, actions, and desires.

How can the Scriptures, prayer, the sacraments, and the example of other Christians help you to be chaste?

LONGANIMITY (Long-suffering) The love of a friend can ease pain. Belief in God's love for you can help you endure pain over a long period of time.

MILDNESS Strength tempered by love leads you to be gentle, peaceful, and gracious. A mild person has the power to forgive instead of getting angry.

Louise wrapped a white scarf around her head and tied on a clean apron. Then she scrubbed her hands with vinegar. She picked up a stack of linens and headed for the first hospital bed. Memories filled her mind. Vincent de Paul had to persuade Church authorities to let the Daughters of Charity work outside the convent. This was something new in seventeenth-century Europe. When Louise scraped together money, it was only enough to buy the Hotel Dieu, a hospital known as a rat hole.

The first volunteers who joined Louise were rich ladies. Horrified at the sights and smells of the sick and the poor, they quit. Louise was disappointed but peaceful. She found other women who were generous and loved Christ in the poor. They scrubbed, sewed, painted, cooked, and prayed until they had a suitable hospital. The problems were not over, however. There were bills to pay. The needs were overwhelming, and the work was hard and often discouraging. But after each disappointment, Louise would go to chapel. She would emerge with a big smile. She knew that it was foolish to get upset. God's love conquers all. It just takes time.

PRACTICE! What is your reaction when you are disappointed? Do you become discouraged?

What does St. Louise de Marillac teach you?

WORKS AND FRUITS
The fruits of the Spirit are all forms of love. They are shown in the works of mercy. Write two works and a fruit that would be shown in each.

_____

_____

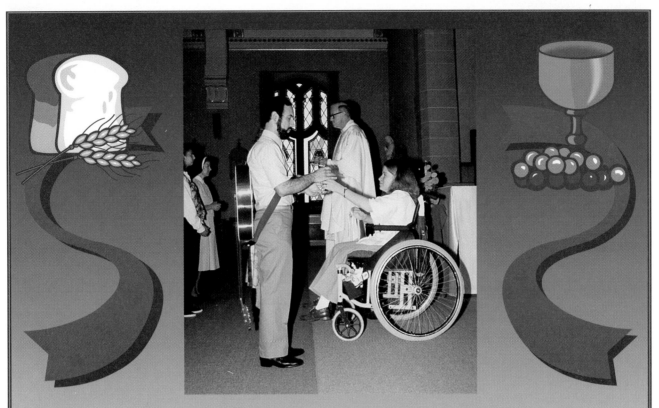

VIRGINIA VONTORCIK: A WOMAN WITH A MISSION

Virginia Vontorcik knows what she wants to do in life. Open to the Spirit working in her, she has reflected on her own life experiences and has decided to be a pastoral counselor. In particular she would like to nurture the faith of children and young adults who are hospitalized. Her desire is to help them keep their faith and help it grow in whatever situation they find themselves. It was in a hospital that Virginia learned to appreciate her own faith.

Because she has spina bifida, during junior high school Virginia underwent a series of operations. She spent the greater part of eighteen months in the hospital. During this time she was separated from the Church. No one from the parish community came to visit her, and only once was she able to receive Communion. Without support, Virginia lost her faith and entered a dark and painful period of her life.

When Virginia returned home, her parents insisted that she go to Mass with them. During that first Mass, at Communion time, the Spirit led Virginia to realize what she had been missing. She was renewed in faith, and the Eucharist became very special to her.

In hopes of preventing others from suffering the loss she experienced, Virginia is working toward her goal of being a pastoral counselor. She is taking psychology and theology courses in college. She is also enrolled in the Stephen ministry at the local parish. After fifty hours of training, she will be paired with someone in the parish who needs help during a crisis period. She has made a two-year commitment to serve in this way.

Virginia is also a eucharistic minister. In her ministry the Eucharist will be her source of strength, and she will find joy in bringing it to others who are in need.

Countless numbers of people like Virginia are using their gifts and devoting themselves to Church ministry. Through them the Spirit continues to renew the face of the earth.

Judging from your life experiences and your gifts, what kind of Church ministry would you be good at?

_____

_____

REMEMBER

How can we recognize the fruits of the Spirit?
We can recognize the fruits of the Spirit in ourselves by the happiness we experience in doing good. Others become aware of the Spirit's presence in us by witnessing our good works.

Words to Know

◆ fruits of the Spirit

Words to Memorize

The fruits of the Spirit

RESPOND

Choose a fruit of the Spirit. List ways you can show that fruit. Write a prayer asking for the grace of living that fruit.

REACH OUT

1. Look up other signs of the Spirit found in 1 Timothy 3:9; 4:12; 6:11; 2 Timothy 2:22, 24; 1 Peter 1:5–7; 1 Peter 3:8; and Ephesians 5:9. Write how these are evident in your parish community. Offer to include some of your thoughts in the parish bulletin.
2. Make a book jacket for the story of your patron saint. On the back cover, give the fruits of the Spirit evident in the life of this saint and how they were shown.
3. The *mystagogy* is a period after initiation to reflect on the Christian mysteries and the sacraments celebrated. Participate in the Eucharist with your parents, your sponsor, and the other newly confirmed. Afterwards, share refreshments. Discuss insights you have had in living as a Christian.
4. Show your confessor the "Plan for Growth" you have made. Follow his suggestions for ways you can develop your spiritual life.
5. As a fully initiated Christian, you will be thinking about your mission or vocation in life. Interview a single person, a married couple (your parents), and a religious or priest about how they have experienced their call.

REVIEW

Searching for Fruit   Circle the twelve fruits of the Spirit in the word search. Be able to explain how they can be found in a Christian life.

```
W M O D E S T Y T C I N
C Z A E S N B G W H B L
O G O O D N E S S A S O
N J M I L D N E S S K F
T R P T E U I H C T M A
I X E J F L G V H I N I
N P A T I E N C E T J T
E I C H A R I T Y Y C H
N P E Q F M T U P M K I
C T G X J O Y C Y O A T
E L O N G A N I M I T Y
```

Name the Fruit   Write the letter of the fruit that each person described could especially use.

a. charity	e. benignity	i. faith
b. joy	f. goodness	j. modesty
c. peace	g. longanimity	k. continence
d. patience	h. mildness	l. chastity

_____   1. Jittery Jan
_____   2. Boastful Bob
_____   3. Self-centered Sue
_____   4. Mean Mike
_____   5. Gloomy Gloria
_____   6. Hotheaded Harry
_____   7. Lustful Larry
_____   8. Whining Wanda
_____   9. Self-indulgent Sally
_____ 10. Impatient Patty
_____ 11. Evil Evelyn
_____ 12. Irresponsible Rudy

Thumbnail Sketch of a Christian   Write three sentences that describe a Christian your age.

_____

_____

_____

_____

_____

Mystagogy Manual

You are now a fully initiated Christian. It's time to walk the talk, to live out the commitment you ratified in Confirmation. You can start by imitating the last phase of the RCIA called mystagogy. **Mystagogy** is the learning and the deepening of faith that occurs after initiation during the five weeks between the Easter Vigil and Pentecost. The mystery the candidates were initiated into becomes a vibrant part of their lives. With the community that welcomed them, they meditate on the Gospels of these weeks, share in the Eucharist, and do works of charity.

Your initiation into the Church has given you an equal share with all other Christians in the dignity of being a member and in the responsibility to build up the Church. You belong to the universal Church, but you live out your commitment in your local parish and diocese. The most important contribution you can make to the Church is to live out your life in a holy manner so that others "seeing your good works . . . may give praise to your Father in heaven" (Matthew 5:16 JB).

Christ was anointed for his work as priest, prophet, and king. You are anointed in Baptism and Confirmation to carry on his work.

You accept your **priestly** role by
- being the way, discovering the way, or inventing the way Christian teaching and life influence the world in which you are
- making everything you do and your sufferings and joys a spiritual sacrifice
- consecrating the world to God and bringing it back into union with its creator by leading a holy life.

You accept your **prophetic** role by
- using your intelligence and the Spirit's gifts to find ways for the values of the Beatitudes to influence government, business, and society
- witnessing to the faith by living and teaching it, bringing Gospel teachings into places, using the media, and working with parish organizations
- spreading the message of salvation.

You accept your **kingly** role by
- using your gifts to bring all to the kingdom of God
- overcoming sin and controlling habits that lead to sin
- joining with others to remedy conditions that cause people to sin
- serving the Church by accepting ministries for which your gifts qualify you.

The Church needs you and is pleased that you have completed your initiation. How will you help carry out its mission? You must think, pray, and plan. Consider what jobs are open to you in your parish and their qualifications. Assess your God-given gifts. A chart to help you follows. Circle the number that fits you on the scale in each area; 1 is weak and 5 is strong. Your strengths will suggest what you are called and gifted to do.

MENTAL

intelligence: I acquire and apply knowledge of the world about me.

1   2   3   4   5

discernment: I interpret correctly evidence presented to me in my spiritual life and the world around me.

1   2   3   4   5

memory: I store and recall past experience

1   2   3   4   5

creativity: I imagine original ways of saying, doing, and arranging to bring about something new.

1   2   3   4   5

reasonableness: I act from conviction rather than emotions on issues.

1   2   3   4   5

comprehension: I grasp and understand events and their consequences.

1   2   3   4   5

alertness: I am attentive and mentally vigilant to situations that affect my life.

1   2   3   4   5

EMOTIONAL

I am warm, approachable.

1   2   3   4   5

I am consistent, dependable.

1   2   3   4   5

I am patient, enduring.

1   2   3   4   5

I am cheerful, enthusiastic.

1   2   3   4   5

I am adaptable.

1   2   3   4   5

I am hopeful.

1   2   3   4   5

I am supportive, caring.

1   2   3   4   5

SPIRITUAL

dedication: I remain committed to my faith and relationships with friends even when it is difficult. I am loyal to God and God's laws, and I strive to be dependable.

1   2   3   4   5

humility: I know my strengths and weaknesses and don't cover them up or brag about the good I have done.

1   2   3   4   5

self-discipline: I am able to control my temper, impulses, and loves in my life so that they all work together for my spiritual good.

1   2   3   4   5

compassion: I am alert and sensitive to the needs of others. I rejoice when others succeed and comfort them when things do not turn out well.

1   2   3   4   5

honesty: I am truthful in what I say and omit saying. The laws of God and my community guide me in my dealings with others' property and possessions. I readily admit when I am wrong.

1   2   3   4   5

leadership ability: I temper my enthusiasm and wait for God's time to act instead of insisting on my way. I recognize God has given me intelligence, good judgment, and a pleasing personality to use in working with others. I never give up working for a good cause even when it demands a struggle.

1   2   3   4   5

GIFTS OF THE SPIRIT

wisdom: I appreciate the help God gives me in judging persons, places, and things.

1   2   3   4   5

understanding: I have insight into what my faith means and the demands it makes on how I should live. I strive to increase this gift by prayer and study.

1   2   3   4   5

counsel: I have set my life in order and can advise others. I am open to good advice from parents and friends.

1   2   3   4   5

knowledge: I value all things in terms of how they affect my relationship with God, whom I know as my friend and highest good.

1   2   3   4   5

courage: I am able to take a moral stand on issues even when it makes me unpopular. I am faithful in everyday duties.

1   2   3   4   5

reverence: I love God and am developing a deeper friendship with God as well as a respect for all creation. Prayer is a habit with me.

1   2   3   4   5

wonder and awe: I constantly marvel at all God's gifts to me. I intend to love, obey, and trust God always.

1   2   3   4   5

FRUITS OF THE SPIRIT

love: I am quick to sense the needs of others and respond.

1   2   3   4   5

faithfulness: I stick to my promises. I can be counted on to be firm in my commitment to God and others.

1   2   3   4   5

joy: I can celebrate life even in the midst of pain and confusion because I experience the presence of God.

1   2   3   4   5

modesty: I have a right understanding of my abilities and do not boast or act in an extreme manner to gain attention.

1   2   3   4   5

kindness: I act towards others as I want them to act toward me. I try to see the best in them.

1   2   3   4   5

goodness: I desire to let God's goodness shine out to others. An inner strength permits me to be gentle. I do not abuse authority delegated to me.

1   2   3   4   5

peace: I have a quiet, inner confidence in God's care of me that keeps me from feeling uptight and anxious.

1   2   3   4   5

patience: I can handle frustration and conflict without giving up. I am willing to endure sufferings, delays, and routine.

1   2   3   4   5

self-control: I am learning to live with my limitations. I discipline the use of my time and do not let my sexual powers get out of control. I am in control of my emotions.

1   2   3   4   5

chastity: I can control my sexual powers and live chastely according to my state in life because I love and respect myself and others.

1   2   3   4   5

long suffering: My belief in God enables me to endure pain and disappointment over a long period of time because I know that I do not suffer alone.

1   2   3   4   5

mildness: I can control myself and be peaceful and gracious in forgiving even when it is hard to do.

1   2   3   4   5

The Ten Commandments

1. I, the Lord, am your God. You shall not have other gods besides me.
2. You shall not take the name of the Lord, your God, in vain.
3. Remember to keep holy the Sabbath day.
4. Honor your father and your mother.
5. You shall not kill.
6. You shall not commit adultery.
7. You shall not steal.
8. You shall not bear false witness against your neighbor.
9. You shall not covet your neighbor's wife.
10. You shall not covet anything that belongs to your neighbor.

Duties of a Catholic Christian

1. To keep holy the day of the Lord's resurrection (Sunday). To worship God by participating in Mass for every Sunday and holy day of obligation. To avoid those activities (like needless work) that would hinder worship, joy, or relaxation.
2. To lead a sacramental life. To receive Holy Communion frequently and the Sacrament of Reconciliation regularly.
3. To study Catholic teachings in preparation for the Sacrament of Confirmation, to be confirmed, and then to continue to study and advance the cause of Christ.
4. To observe the marriage laws of the Church. To give religious training, by word and example, to one's children. To use parish schools and catechetical programs.
5. To strengthen and support the Church— one's own parish community and parish priests, the worldwide Church, and the pope.
6. To do penance, including abstaining from meat and fasting from food on the appointed days.
7. To join in the missionary spirit and apostolate of the Church.

Days of Fast (for adults)

Ash Wednesday   Good Friday

Days of Abstinence (for all those over age 14)

Ash Wednesday   All Fridays in Lent

Holy Days of Obligation in the United States

Solemnity of Mary, Mother of God: January 1
We honor Mary, Mother of God.

Ascension: Fortieth day after Easter
Jesus ascended into heaven.

Assumption: August 15
Mary was taken into heaven, body and soul.

All Saints' Day: November 1
We honor all the saints in heaven.

Immaculate Conception: December 8
Mary was free from sin from the first moment of her life.

Christmas: December 25
We celebrate the birth of Jesus.

The Seven Sacraments

Baptism, Confirmation, Eucharist, Reconciliation (Penance), Anointing of the Sick, Matrimony, Holy Orders

Corporal Works of Mercy

Feed the hungry
Give drink to the thirsty
Clothe the naked
Visit the sick
Shelter the homeless
Visit the imprisoned
Bury the dead

Spiritual Works of Mercy

Warn the sinner
Instruct the ignorant
Counsel the doubtful
Comfort the sorrowing
Bear wrongs patiently
Forgive all injuries
Pray for the living and the dead

The Theological Virtues

Faith, hope, love (charity)

The Cardinal Virtues

Prudence, temperance, justice, fortitude

The Beatitudes (Matthew 5:3–10)

Blessed are the poor in spirit, for theirs is the kingdom of heaven.

Blessed are they who mourn, for they will be comforted.

Blessed are the meek, for they will inherit the land.

Blessed are they who hunger and thirst for righteousness, for they will be satisfied.

Blessed are the merciful, for they will be shown mercy.

Blessed are the clean of heart, for they will see God.

Blessed are the peacemakers, for they will be called children of God.

Blessed are they who are persecuted for the sake of righteousness, for theirs is the kingdom of heaven.

The Way of the Cross

I. Jesus is condemned to death on the cross.
II. Jesus accepts his cross.
III. Jesus falls the first time.
IV. Jesus meets his sorrowful mother.
V. Simon of Cyrene helps Jesus carry his cross.
VI. Veronica wipes the face of Jesus.
VII. Jesus falls the second time.
VIII. Jesus meets and speaks to the women of Jerusalem.
IX. Jesus falls the third time.
X. Jesus is stripped of his garments.
XI. Jesus is nailed to the cross.
XII. Jesus dies on the cross.
XIII. Jesus is taken down from the cross and laid in his mother's arms.
XIV. Jesus is placed in the tomb.
XV. Jesus rises from the dead.

Gifts of the Holy Spirit

Wisdom, understanding, right judgment (counsel), courage (fortitude), knowledge, reverence (piety), wonder and awe (fear of the Lord)

Fruits of the Holy Spirit

charity	benignity	faith
joy	goodness	modesty
peace	longanimity	continency
patience	mildness	chastity

The Mysteries of the Rosary

Joyful Mysteries

The Annunciation
The Visitation
The Nativity
The Presentation in the Temple
The Finding of Jesus in the Temple

Sorrowful Mysteries

The Agony in the Garden
The Scourging at the Pillar
The Crowning with Thorns
The Carrying of the Cross
The Crucifixion and Death of Jesus

Glorious Mysteries

The Resurrection
The Ascension
The Descent of the Holy Spirit
The Assumption of Mary
The Crowning of Mary as Queen of Heaven and Earth

The Divine Praises

Blessed be God.
Blessed be his holy name.
Blessed be Jesus Christ, true God and true man.
Blessed be the name of Jesus.
Blessed be his most Sacred Heart.
Blessed be his most Precious Blood.
Blessed be Jesus in the most Holy Sacrament of the Altar.
Blessed be the Holy Spirit, the Paraclete.
Blessed be the great Mother of God, Mary most holy.
Blessed be her holy and Immaculate Conception.
Blessed be her glorious Assumption.
Blessed be the name of Mary, Virgin and Mother.
Blessed be St. Joseph, her most chaste spouse.
Blessed be God in his angels and in his saints.

GLOSSARY

A

Absolution (AB suh LOO shun): Forgiveness or pardon for sin. In the Sacrament of Reconciliation, the priest acts with God's power to give absolution.

Abstain (ab STAYN): To refrain from an action such as eating certain foods. Catholics fourteen years and older are bound by the law of abstinence.

Anointing (Uh NOYNT ing): The act of consecrating a person or a thing by applying blessed oil or chrism.

Apostolic (AP uh STOL ik): That identifying mark or gift of the Church by which the pope and all bishops can trace their priestly leadership and teachings back to Jesus and the apostles.

B

Baptism (BAP tiz um): The first of the seven sacraments by which one receives divine life, is cleansed of all sin by rebirth in Christ, and is incorporated into the Church; one of the sacraments of initiation.

Beatitudes (bee AT uh toods): In Matthew's Gospel a set of guidelines for Christlike living that will make us happy and lead us to eternal life. In each Beatitude a value is paired with a promise.

Bishop (BISH up): An ordained priest appointed by the pope who has received the fullness of Christ's priesthood through the prayers and the imposition of a consecrating bishop's hands; a successor of the apostles whose sphere of authority is a diocese.

Body of Christ: The Church; the union of all Christians with Christ and with one another. This union is initiated in Baptism and is strengthened by prayer, the other sacraments, and the practice of virtue.

C

Canon Law: Official rules that guide all aspects of Church life.

Capital sins: Seven evil tendencies that are the source of all sins: pride, covetousness, lust, anger, gluttony, envy, and sloth.

Cardinal moral virtues: Powers given at baptism that help us to act the right way: prudence, justice, fortitude, and temperance.

Catholic: That identifying mark or gift of the Church that enables her to teach the total message of Jesus to all people everywhere and in every age.

Character: The indelible, invisible mark or seal that a person receives at Baptism, Confirmation, and Holy Orders. It consecrates the person in such a manner that these sacraments may be received only once.

Charism (KAIR iz um): A special gift given by the Holy Spirit to an individual member of the Church for the good of the entire Church; charismatic gifts.

Chrism: A blessed mixture of olive (or plant) oil and balsam (or perfume) used in anointing during Baptism, Confirmation, and Holy Orders. Chrism is usually consecrated at the Mass of Chrism on Holy Thursday.

Church: God's faithful people; the Mystical Body of Christ; a community of believers; the human and divine society in which Christ is alive and acting in the world today.

Communion of saints: The Church on Earth, in heaven, and in purgatory.

Community: A group of people who share the same beliefs, live together, and work to benefit one another and others. Members of a Christian community are bound by their love for Christ and for one another and by their Spirit-guided service to the world.

Confirmation (CON fur MAY shun): One of the seven sacraments by which a baptized Christian is sealed with the gift of the Holy Spirit and is bound more closely to the Church; one of the sacraments of initiation. Confirmation obliges one to love, study, defend, and spread the faith.

Contrition (Kun TRISH un): True sorrow for sin with the intention not to sin again. Contrition includes conversion, a resolution to change one's life according to Jesus' teachings.

Covenant (KUV uh nunt): A sacred contract; a holy agreement; a solemn, binding pact between two or more persons; here between God and God's people.

Creed: A statement or prayer listing religious beliefs. The Apostles' Creed and the Nicene Creed are prayers that list Catholic religious beliefs.

D

Discernment (dih SURN ment): The process of coming to see God's will in a decision through prayer, reflection, and consultation.

Dogma (DAWG muh): Any truth or doctrine of the Church that has been revealed in Scripture or Tradition and defined by the Church. Catholics must believe in dogmas.

E

Ecumenism (eh KYOO muh nizm): A movement that aims to restore Christian unity.

Eucharist (YOO kuh rist): The sacrament of the Body and Blood of Christ; a sacrifice of love and a sacred meal. The Eucharist is the fullness of Christian initiation.

Evangelization (ih VAN juh liz AY shun): The act of proclaiming the Good News of Jesus, especially to people who have not yet heard it.

Examination of conscience: Prayerful reflection on one's relationship with God, a review of one's observance of God's laws.

Excommunication: Separation from the Church, especially the Eucharist, as a result of not practicing its beliefs.

F

Faith: A free gift of God by which we believe and trust him and believe all that his Church teaches.

Fast: To take only one full meal and two lighter meals a day and no food between meals. Catholics must fast on Ash Wednesday and Good Friday from their 21st birthday to their 59th.

Fruits of the Holy Spirit: Supernatural works that result from and manifest the presence of the Holy Spirit. The traditional list includes charity, joy, peace, patience, kindness, goodness, longanimity, benignity, faith, modesty, chastity, and continency.

G

Gifts of the Holy Spirit: Supernatural habits that perfect the soul beyond the virtues enabling one to be ready and responsive to divine grace. The seven gifts are wisdom, understanding, right judgment (counsel), knowledge, courage (fortitude), reverence (piety), and wonder and awe (fear of the Lord).

H

Heaven: The place and state of perfect, eternal happiness that belongs to those who have loved and served God on Earth. The blessed in heaven see God face-to-face and forever know, love, and enjoy God and other saints.

Heresy (HAIR eh see): A religious belief that opposes or denies any divinely revealed truth of the Catholic faith.

Holiness: That gift, or mark, of the Church that identifies her as saintly or virtuous. The Church is holy because she has a holy founder, teaches a holy doctrine, and produces holy persons through the Mass and the sacraments. Individuals are holy if they lead saintly lives of love and service of God and neighbor.

Holy day of obligation: A special feast that Catholics are bound to celebrate by participating in the Eucharist.

Holy Spirit: God, the Third Person of the Blessed Trinity; the Paraclete (helper) or Advocate whom Jesus promised to send after his ascension. The promise was fulfilled on Pentecost.

I

Imposition of hands (IM puh ZISH un): The laying on of hands to invoke God and his blessing. The imposition of hands is a part of the Rite of Confirmation.

Infallibility (in fal ih BIL ih tee): One of the traits of the Catholic Church whereby it is free from error when teaching matters of faith or morals.

J

Journal: Any book in which are recorded one's reflections on life, including one's growing relationship with the Lord.

L

Liturgical Year (lih TUR jih kul): The annual cycle during which the Church celebrates the whole mystery of Christ (i.e., his Paschal Mystery) and honors Mary, the angels, and the saints. These mysteries are celebrated in the Mass, the Liturgy of the Hours, and other acts of public worship.

Liturgy of the Hours: The extension of the praise and worship of the Eucharist into certain hours of the day by Scripture, prayers, and spiritual reading; the official, unending public prayer of the universal Church.

M

Magisterium (MA jis TAIR ee um): The special teaching authority of the Church.

Mark: Any of the four distinguishing characteristics of the Catholic Church: one, holy, catholic, apostolic.

Mortal sin: A serious offense against God that destroys our friendship with him and causes us to lose grace and eternal life.

O

One: Complete and undivided. The Church's mark or gift of oneness or unity means that she has only one founder, Jesus Christ; one visible ruler, the pope; one act of worship and one sacramental system; and one set of doctrines.

P

Paraclete (PAIR uh kleet): One who gives witness to another; one who defends or helps another; an advocate; one of the titles of the Holy Spirit.

Paschal Mystery: The suffering, death, resurrection, and ascension of Jesus through which humankind was saved from sin and death.

Penance/Reconciliation (PEN uns / REK un sil ee AY shun): The sacrament through which our sins are forgiven and we are reconciled or made one with God, the community, and ourselves.

Pentecost (PEN teh kawst): The fiftieth day after Easter on which the Holy Spirit came upon Jesus' followers in the fulfillment of his promise; the birthday of the Church, its public manifestation.

Pope: The visible leader of the Catholic Church on Earth; a successor of St. Peter the Apostle; the bishop of Rome; the chief bishop; the Vicar of Christ.

Prayer: A conscious and deliberate turning toward God; a lifting up of the mind and heart to God; conversation or communion with God.

Purgatory (PUR ga TOR ee): The temporary state of the dead who must still be purified from sin before entering heaven. The souls in purgatory are holy. We pray for them and may ask them to pray for us.

R

Rite of Christian Initiation of Adults (RCIA): The process that leads a non-Christian adult to full communion with the Catholic Church.

S

Sacrifice (SAK rih fys): An offering made to God of a person or of a thing, such as an animal or farm products, in adoration; an act of self-denial, often prompted by love of God.

Sacrament: An outward sign of an inward grace instituted by Christ in which we encounter him at key points in our journey of life.

Saint: A person who cooperated with the graces of the Spirit and lived a Christlike life on Earth and so now enjoys life with God in heaven forever.

Sanctifying grace (SANK tih FY ing): Divine life; God dwelling within us to make us holy.

Scripture: Sacred writings containing God's revelation; the Old Testament (Hebrew Scriptures) and New Testament (Christian Scriptures).

Seal: A stamp or identifying mark that sets aside or consecrates a person or an object for a special mission. (*See* Character.)

Service: Any religious or social work based on the spiritual or the corporal works of mercy.

Sin: An action or omission that is an offense against God's law; it breaks or weakens the unity of the Church.

Sponsor (SPON sur): A practicing Catholic who presents a candidate for Baptism or Confirmation. The sponsor's duty is to support the candidate in living the faith and to give good example in this regard.

T

Theologian: Someone who studies the truths of our faith and tries to understand and explain them better.

Theological virtues: The powers received at Baptism that help us direct our life toward God: faith, hope, and love (charity).

Tradition: Christian beliefs that have been passed down by word, teaching, customs, and example.

Trinity (TRIN uh tee): The central doctrine and mystery that in God there are three persons (God the Father, God the Son, and God the Holy Spirit) with one nature. The Three Persons of the Trinity are equal but distinct.

U

United States Catholic Conference (U.S.C.C.): An organization of bishops that carries out the social teachings of the Church.

V

Vatican City: An independent state of 108 acres in Rome where the pope resides and the administrative offices are located.

Vatican Council II: A 1962–1965 worldwide meeting of bishops called by Pope John XXIII to renew the Church and adapt it to modern times.

Venial sin (VEEN yel): An offense that weakens but does not destroy our relationship with God.

W

Witness: One whose life, words, and actions give testimony to his or her beliefs. The word *martyr* comes from the Greek and means "witness."

Works of mercy: The traditional forms of Christian service to others. The seven spiritual works minister to the soul or spirit. The seven corporal works minister to the body. (*See* Matthew 25:35–40.)

INDEX

CONFIRMATION NOVENA

DAY 6

I give you a new heart, a new spirit within you.

Prayer: May the Spirit strengthen us with courage to accept suffering with faith. Let our prayers comfort the dying and bring all the deceased to eternal life. Let us pray:

    All: Come, Holy Spirit!

Practice: Do not complain, but speak positively.

DAY 7

One Lord, one faith, one Baptism. One God and Father of all.

Prayer: May the Holy Spirit protect and unite the Church. Let our parish family gather for the Eucharist as a community of love. Let us pray:

    All: Come, Holy Spirit!

Practice: Be kind to someone you dislike.

DAY 8

You are God's temple and the Spirit of the Lord lives in you.

Prayer: May the gift of wonder and awe enable us to reject sin, and may the Spirit of the Lord live in us as his temple.

    All: Come, Holy Spirit!

Practice: Try to do only the things that please God.

DAY 9

The Lord has done great things for us; we are filled with joy.

Prayer: On this day of Confirmation, may we be filled with zeal to proclaim the Gospel. In the joy and strength of the Holy Spirit, we pray:

    All: Come, Holy Spirit!

Practice: Be pleasant and grateful to all.

Dear Candidate,

As the day of your confirmation draws near, you will want to take time to reflect on what it means to live in the Spirit of Jesus. One way to do this is by making a novena. A *novena* is nine days of prayer. It has its origin in the nine days Mary and the disciples spent in prayer before the coming of the Spirit on Pentecost.

Making this novena could be one of the most important things you do to prepare for Confirmation. If you come before the Lord truly open to his Spirit at work in your heart, you will receive special graces. You will discover more about God's great love for you and be ready to respond to his love as a confirmed Christian.

Each day, read the thought taken from Scripture and pray the prayer. Then try to do the practice for the intention stated in the prayer. Ask others to pray for you and with you, as you prepare to be a confirmed Catholic who brings God's love to others.

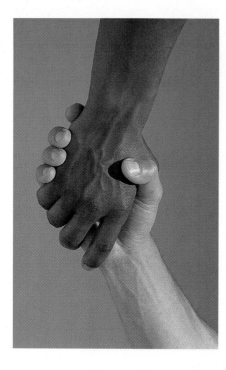

DAY 1
Lord, send out your Spirit and renew the face of the earth.

Prayer: May the Holy Spirit reconcile all divisions in friendships, families, nations, and the Church. May the gift of knowledge help us work for peace. Let us pray:
All: Come, Holy Spirit!
Practice: Seek forgiveness if necessary, or pray a prayer for peace in a particular country.

DAY 2
Come, Holy Spirit, shine on us with the radiance of your love.

Prayer: May the Holy Spirit help us to rejoice in the countless blessings God has given us and teach us to do God's will. May the Spirit's wisdom guide us and all God's people. Let us pray:
All: Come, Holy Spirit!
Practice: Spend extra time in silent prayer, talking and listening to the Spirit in your heart.

DAY 3
We follow Christ, who was anointed by the Spirit to bring us good news.

Prayer: May the Holy Spirit give us right judgment to act justly: to release oppressed people, to shelter the homeless, to see Christ in the poor, and to comfort those who mourn. Let us pray:
All: Come, Holy Spirit!
Practice: Earn or set aside money for a charitable cause.

DAY 4
The Father will send the Holy Spirit to be with you always.

Prayer: May the Holy Spirit fill our hearts with love for the Father and respect for creation. May the gift of reverence enable us to respect and develop nature and not destroy it. Let us pray:
All: Come, Holy Spirit!
Practice: Use everything with care today.

DAY 5
When the Spirit of truth comes, he will teach you all truth.

Prayer: May the Spirit's gift of understanding enlighten us to grasp better Christ's love for us and show us how to love others as he loves us. May we show our love by serving our brothers and sisters. Let us pray:
All: Come, Holy Spirit!
Practice: Do someone a hidden favor today.

EXAMINATION OF CONSCIENCE

◆ Is God first in my life? Have I neglected to pray? Refused to participate at the Eucharist? Missed Mass? Arrived late? Received Communion without any preparation or thanksgiving?
◆ Do I show respect for God's name? Do I use it when I am angry, acting big, or being silly?
◆ Have I been obedient to my parents? Loving toward them? Have I ignored them? Caused them to worry because of my activities? Quarreled with my brothers or sisters?
◆ Have I tried to bring family peace?
◆ Have I respected teachers and others in authority?
◆ Have I harmed my body by improper diet? Use of alcohol? Use of drugs?
◆ Do I keep my mind clean and healthy? Have I read, listened to, or related impure stories? Have I used my genital organs for my own pleasure?
◆ Have I shown respect for the opposite sex?
◆ Have I lied? Ruined the reputation of another person? Have I been jealous? Angry with others? Have I refused to ask forgiveness? Treated another coldly? Made fun of others?
◆ Do I take care of my things? Do I save natural resources?
◆ Have I cheated at games or on tests? Damaged or stolen property without making restitution? Failed to help the poor?
◆ What is keeping me from being the person Jesus expects me to be?

A DAILY PLAN TO FOLLOW

1. Read and reflect on a Scripture passage. (Matthew 5:23-24 Whom do I need to forgive to help form a more united community?)
2. Examine your conscience. Use the questions on the next page.
3. Pray an act of contrition.
My God,
I am sorry for my sins with all my heart.
In choosing to do wrong,
and failing to do good,
I have sinned against you
whom I should love above all things.
I firmly intend with your help,
to do penance,
to sin no more,
and to avoid whatever leads me to sin.
Our Savior Jesus Christ
suffered and died for us.
In his name, my God, have mercy.
from Rite of Reconciliation
4. Plan for the future.
I must sincerely intend to change my life and live according to the teachings of Jesus. What resolution will I make?

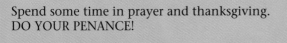

THE RITE OF RECONCILIATION
◆ Greet the priest.
◆ Make the Sign of the Cross.
◆ Listen as the priest prays.
◆ Read or listen to the Word of God (optional).
◆ Confess your sins. (Mention how long it has been since your last confession. For mortal sin, tell how often it has occurred.)
◆ Speak about anything that is troubling you.
◆ Listen to the priest's advice.
◆ Accept your penance.
◆ Pray an act of contrition. (You may use your own words.)
◆ Receive absolution, silently making the Sign of the Cross. Respond, "Amen."
◆ Proclamation of praise and dismissal:
Priest: Give thanks to the Lord, for he is good.
Response: His mercy endures forever.
◆ Say, "Thank you, Father."

Spend some time in prayer and thanksgiving.
DO YOUR PENANCE!

A clean heart create for me, God;
renew in me a steadfast spirit.

Psalm 51:12

Name:

Faith Makes a Difference

Respond to each statement by circling the corresponding number:

1 = Never   2 = Seldom   3 = Frequently   4 = Always

I believe in God, the Father almighty,

I pray to God. 1 2 3 4

I try to learn about God by studying and listening to homilies. 1 2 3 4

I worship God at Sunday Masses. 1 2 3 4

I care for others as my brothers and sisters. 1 2 3 4

creator of heaven and earth,

I handle the things of Earth as gifts from God. 1 2 3 4

I share what I have with others. 1 2 3 4

I believe in Jesus Christ, his only Son, our Lord.

I read the Bible and pray about it. 1 2 3 4

I try to build my relationship with Christ. 1 2 3 4

I model my life on Jesus. 1 2 3 4

I show reverence at Mass and Holy Communion. 1 2 3 4

He was conceived by the power of the Holy Spirit and born of the Virgin Mary.

I pray to Mary, my heavenly mother. 1 2 3 4

I honor Mary in special ways. 1 2 3 4

He suffered under Pontius Pilate, was crucified, died, and was buried. He descended to the dead.

I show gratitude to God for redeeming me. 1 2 3 4

I unite my suffering with Christ's, and I offer it for a good intention. 1 2 3 4

On the third day he rose again. He ascended into heaven, and is seated at the right hand of the Father. He will come again to judge the living and the dead.

I obey the commandments. 1 2 3 4

I practice the works of mercy. 1 2 3 4

I encourage my friends to do good and avoid evil. 1 2 3 4

I try to improve my practice of virtue. 1 2 3 4

I believe in the Holy Spirit,

I turn to the Holy Spirit in time of need. 1 2 3 4

I am preparing well for Confirmation. 1 2 3 4

the holy catholic Church, the communion of saints,

I try to increase my knowledge of the Church's teachings. 1 2 3 4

I participate in parish activities. 1 2 3 4

I try to share my faith with others. 1 2 3 4

I pray to the saints and for those in purgatory. 1 2 3 4

I am kind to others. 1 2 3 4

the forgiveness of sins,

I make use of the Sacrament of Penance. 1 2 3 4

I pray an act of contrition every night. 1 2 3 4

the resurrection of the body, and life everlasting.

I take care of my body. 1 2 3 4

I treat my body, and the bodies of others, with respect. 1 2 3 4

I give evidence of my faith in eternal life by praying for those who have died and by attending wakes and funerals. 1 2 3 4

You have struck our hearts with your love, and like arrows that stick in the heart, we bear your words in us.

St. Augustine

Truly, this is my hope and my only comfort—to fly to you in every trouble, to trust steadfastly in you, to call inwardly upon you, and to abide patiently in your coming and your heavenly consoler, which, I trust, will quickly come to me.

Thomas à Kempis

You, eternal Trinity, are a deep sea: the more I enter you, the more I discover, the more I seek.

St. Catherine of Siena

Father, I abandon myself into your hands; do with me what you will. Whatever you may do, I thank you: I am ready for all, I accept all. Let only your will be done in me and in all your creatures—I wish no more than this, Lord.

Venerable Charles de Foucauld

Most high, glorious God, enlighten the darkness of my heart and give me, Lord, a correct faith, a certain hope, a perfect charity, sense and knowledge, so that I may carry out your holy and true command.

St. Francis of Assisi

You are medicine for me when I am sick;
You are my strength when I need help;
You are life itself when I fear death;
You are the way when I long for heaven;
You are light when all is dark;
You are my food when I need nourishment!

St. Ambrose

O gracious and holy Father,
Give us wisdom to perceive you,
intelligence to understand you,
diligence to seek you,
patience to wait for you,
eyes to see you,
a heart to meditate on you,
and a life to proclaim you,
through the power of the Spirit of Jesus Christ our Lord.

St. Benedict

Your pleasure, merciful God—grant that I may desire it ardently, learn it carefully, recognize it truly, fulfill it perfectly, to the praise and glory of your name.

St. Thomas Aquinas

Holy Spirit, Spirit of truth, you are the reward of the saints, the comforter of souls, light in the darkness, riches to the poor, treasure to lovers, food for the hungry, comfort to those who are wandering; to sum up, you are the one in whom all treasures are contained.

St. Mary Magdelene Dei Pazzi

As in heaven thy will is punctually performed, so may it be done on earth by all creatures, particularly in me and by me.

Elizabeth of Hungary

Lord grant me a holy heart
that sees always what is fine and pure
and is not frightened at the sight of sin,
but creates order wherever it goes.
Grant me a heart that knows nothing
of boredom, weeping, and sighing;
Let me not be too concerned
with the bothersome thing I call "myself."
Lord, give me a sense of humor,
and I will find happiness in life
and profit for others.

St. Thomas More

Before you, Father,
In righteousness and humility,
With you, Brother,
In faith and courage,
In you, Spirit,
In stillness.

Dag Hammarskjöld

O Lord, give me true heavenly wisdom that I may learn to seek you and to find you, and above all things to love you. And to understand and know all other things as they are after the direction of your wisdom, and not otherwise.

Thomas à Kempis

Those things, good Lord, that we pray for,
Give us thy grace to labor for.

Thomas More

O Lord our God, grant us grace to desire you with a whole heart, that so desiring you we may seek and find you, and so finding you may love you, and loving you may hate those sins which separate us from you, for the sake of Jesus Christ. Amen.

St. Anselm

A Prayer Guide for the Journey

WHAT DOES JESUS SAY ABOUT HONESTY?

Matthew 5:33–37

Matthew 6:1–8

WHAT DOES JESUS SAY ABOUT ACCUMULATING POSSESSIONS?

Matthew 6:19–34

Luke 12:13–21

Name: _____

You are preparing to receive the Holy Spirit and the gifts of Confirmation. In order to be open to the graces God offers you in this sacrament, you will want to know Jesus better and try to be more like him. You can do this by spending some extra time with him every day . . . in PRAYER.

The suggestions in this booklet will help you to pray and deepen your relationship with God. Try them TODAY.

MORNING PRAYER

As soon as you wake up, thank God for protecting you during the night and for giving you another day. Offer the new day to God: all that you will do and say, all that the day holds for you, both joys and sufferings. You might offer it for a special intention. You might pray the Morning Offering prayer:

O Jesus, through the immaculate heart of Mary,
I offer you my prayers, works, joys, and sufferings of this day
in union with the holy sacrifice of the Mass throughout the world.
I offer them for all the intentions of your Sacred Heart:
the salvation of souls,
reparation for sin,
the reunion of all Christians.
I offer them for the intentions of our bishops and of all Apostles
of Prayer,
and in particular for those recommended by our Holy Father this
month.

Look ahead to what you expect that day and ask God to help see you through.

MEAL PRAYERS

Before eating, think of God who has provided food. Ask God to bless it. When you are finished eating, thank God for the food and for all the good things your Creator has given you.

NIGHT PRAYER

Before going to bed review your day. Thank God for the good things that happened. Examine your conscience and ask forgiveness for anything you've done that shows a lack of love for God. Pray an act of contrition. Ask God to bless the people you love and anyone in particular who might need God's blessing.

Matthew 23:13–26

Luke 16:19–31

Luke 18:9–14

Matthew 12:9–13

SPECIAL PRAYER TIME

Choose a time that you can give just to God, a time when you are awake, a time when you can be alone and quiet. Plan to spend at least five minutes with the Lord. (Ten or fifteen minutes would be better.)

Find a place that is quiet and private.

Quiet yourself and recall God's presence. Then follow one of these methods of prayer:

I. *Pray aloud some prayers of faith* such as the following:
My God, I believe
  that you are here with me,
  that you love me,
  that you created the whole universe out of love.

Matthew 21:28–32

Jesus, I believe
  that you are the Son of God,
  that you died to save me from sin and death,
  that you rose from the dead and are Lord of Lords.

Holy Spirit, I believe
  that you are the Spirit of life and love,
  that you teach me how to live and love,
  that you will help me to be more like Jesus.

Pray some prayers of praise:
I praise you, Father, for your goodness and love.
I praise you, Jesus, true God and true man, who redeemed the world.
I praise you, Holy Spirit, who inspires me to do good.

(You might pray prayers of thanks or of petition instead.)

Be still and listen to God.
Read a passage in the Bible and think about it.

Luke 19:11–28

Respond: Ask for forgiveness for your sins. Ask for help in living the Christian life in the future. Pray for others.

II. Read a story from the Gospels.
Replay it in your imagination, seeing it as though you were there.
Reflect on what happened and speak to Jesus about it.
Ask what God is saying to you in the passage.
Make a resolution for your life based on the story.

3

10

III. Pray Centering Prayer.

1. *Move toward God within you.* Center, or focus, on God who lives deep within you. Let God's overwhelming love and goodness draw you. Rest in God's presence.

2. *Pray a prayer word or phrase.* Use a prayer, such as "I love you," "My Lord and my God," or simply "Jesus." Repeat it slowly in your mind.

3. *Attend to God and enjoy his presence.* When your mind wanders, use your prayer word to bring you back to giving God your loving attention.

4. *Close with a formal prayer.* Pray the Our Father, Glory to the Father, or another prayer.

IV. Slowly pray a prayer that someone wrote. Reflect on it line by line. A good one for confirmation candidates is "Radiating Christ" by John Henry Newman:

Dear Jesus, help me to spread your fragrance everywhere I go. Flood my soul with your spirit and life; penetrate and possess my whole being so utterly that all my life may only be a radiance of yours. Shine through me and be so in me that every soul I come in contact with may feel your presence in my soul. Let them look up and see no longer me, but only you, Jesus! Stay with me, and I shall begin to shine as you shine, so to shine as a light to others; the light, O Jesus, will be all from you; none of it will be mine. It will be you shining on others through me. Let me thus praise you in the way which you love best—by radiating you to those around me. Let me preach you without preaching, not by my words but by my example, by the catching force, the sympathetic influence of what I do, the evident fullness of the love my heart bears to you.

V. Write your own prayers in your journal and pray them.

VI. Pray prayers in Scripture. Suggestions:
Psalms 1, 4, 8, 13, 16, 19, 23, 25, 33, 34, 42, 46, 51, 62, 63, 77, 84, 86, 91, 96, 103, 111, 121, 138, 139, 145, 150
Isaiah 43:1-3; Isaiah 55:6-11; Daniel 3:52-90; Habakkuk 3:17-19
Luke 1:46-55; Luke 1:68-79
Ephesians 1:3-10; Philippians 2:5-11; Colossians 1:15-21; Revelation 7:10, 12

VII. Pray traditional Catholic prayers: the Rosary, the Way of the Cross.

WHAT DOES JESUS SAY ABOUT WHAT IS IMPORTANT?

Mark 2:23-28

Mark 7:1-23

Mark 10:17-27

Mark 12:13-17

RESPONDING TO JESUS' WORDS

The next pages help you listen to Jesus as he speaks in the Gospels and to respond to him.

WHAT DOES JESUS SAY ABOUT GOD? Read, reflect, and respond.

John 14:1–2

John 16:23–27

Matthew 6:5–13

Luke 5:12–16

Luke 6:27–42

Luke 7:36–50

Matthew 6:25–34

Matthew 10:26–31

Luke 11:5–13

WHAT DOES JESUS SAY ABOUT LOVING OUR NEIGHBOR?

John 15:12

Matthew 18:21–35

Mark 1:23–28

THE SAINTS: OUR COMPANIONS ON THE JOURNEY

The Mendez family has a great devotion to its patron saints. Besides celebrating birthdays, this family celebrates namedays. On July 3, the feast of St. Thomas, for instance, they celebrate Tom's nameday. If possible, the family goes to Mass together that day. Mrs. Mendez prepares Tom's favorite foods. Before they eat, someone prays to St. Thomas for blessings on Tom. The family might even sing a fitting song. One about faith and not seeing but believing would be right for St. Thomas.

Now that your family has a candidate for Confirmation, who is choosing a name and a patron saint, you might reflect on the saints and your relationship to them.

Who Are Saints?

The saints are those who have lived a life of love on Earth and now are with God in heaven enjoying eternal life. We believe that we are bound to them in the Communion of Saints. We pray to them to intercede with God for us. For example, we ask them to pray that we may have the graces we need to live well. We turn to them in special needs. We pray to St. Anthony for help in finding a lost article, to St. Jude for hopeless cases, and to St. Gerard Majella for a successful childbirth. Besides being intercessors for us, the saints are role models. They inspire us by their lives of holiness, they encourage us by proving that it is possible to be holy, and they show us how to go about it.

Saints are all ages, of all nationalities, and from all walks of life. They are fishermen and kings, beggars and lawyers, uneducated peasants and professors, parents and children. Some of the thousands of saints have been canonized, that is, they have been put on the canon, or list, of saints officially declared in heaven by the Church.

How Are Saints Canonized?

At first anyone who was martyred was honored by the early Christians as a saint. Today a local bishop gathers evidence that a person is a saint and submits it to the Congregation for Causes of Saints in Rome. A person is appointed to oversee the writing of an account of the candidate's life. It must be shown that the person lived a life of heroic virtue or was a martyr. Historians and theologians study the document. A board of bishops and cardinals decides whether the person is worthy of being called a saint. If approved, the account is sent to the pope. If the pope approves, the candidate is called venerable. Then if it can be shown that a miracle has been worked through the person's intercession, the pope may declare the person beatified. This means the person is called blessed and people are encouraged to pray to him or her. (No miracles are required for martyrs.) If one more miracle is worked, the candidate may be canonized. Usually this occurs in a Mass in St. Peter's Basilica in Rome. A large picture of the saint is hung in St. Peter's Square.

Many saints have not been canonized either because they are not well known or because no one is that interested in providing the money and backing required for the process. Probably many deceased members of your family are saints in heaven. We celebrate and honor all the saints on All Saints' Day, November 1, which in the United States is a holy day of obligation. Some children dress up on Halloween as one of the saints to call attention to this holiday as the eve of the hallowed (saints).

HOW CAN YOUR FAMILY HONOR THE SAINTS?

Learn to know them.

Saints are becoming more popular. There is much material available on them today. Read books on the lives of the saints so you can talk about them. Bring children's books on the saints into your home. Purchase or rent a video on the life of a saint. Buy sets of cards, the size of playing cards, on the lives of the saints.

Follow the sanctoral cycle, the saint's feast days throughout the year, using a Catholic calendar. Read about the saint of the day and display a picture or statue. (A box of cards, each 6 1/2" by 9", one for each saint of the Church year, is available in the *Saints Kit*, published by Loyola Press.)

In particular find out about the patron saints of your family members, your church, your country. Birthdays and baptism anniversaries are good days to do research on personal patron saints. Become familiar with what the various saints are patrons of. For example, St. Lucy cares for those who have eye problems, St. Francis de Sales is the patron of writers, and St. Joseph is the patron of selling houses.

Pray to them.

At your meal prayers on a saint's feast day add a prayer to him or her. Turn to patron saints in time of need. You might wish to choose a patron saint to care for your family. Remember that the best way we can honor the saints is to imitate their virtues.

Celebrate their feasts.

There are traditional ways to celebrate some of the saints. On the feast of St. Blase, February 3, we get our throats blessed. On St. Valentine's Day, February 14, we exchange love notes. On St. Patrick's Day, March 17, we hold parades, eat green food, and wear shamrocks. On the feast of St. Nicholas, December 6, we find treats (or coal) in our shoes. Find or create ways to celebrate other saints' feasts.

Honor the Queen of All Saints.

Mary, God's Mother, is the greatest of all saints. She was sinless and is already in heaven body and soul. Display her picture or statue somewhere in your home. Visit her shrines. Celebrate her feasts in a special way. During May, the month dedicated to her, pray the rosary and set up a May shrine. On Saturday, the day dedicated to Mary, do something to honor her. During Advent make and display a Mary candle, a white candle with an *M* carved into it and a blue ribbon or cloth around it. Mary, like any good mother, will hear and answer our prayers. She will intercede with her Son for us.

The saints, the friends of God, want to be our friends too! Get to know these good people with whom you hopefully will be spending eternity.